D0513938

Investigating the Twentieth Century

Sources for Local Historians

Investigating the Twentieth Century

Sources for Local Historians

Evelyn Lord

TEMPUS

First published 1999

PUBLISHED IN THE UNITED KINGDOM BY:

Tempus Publishing Ltd
The Mill, Brimscombe Port
Stroud, Gloucestershire GL5 2QG

PUBLISHED IN THE UNITED STATES OF AMERICA BY:

Tempus Publishing Inc.
2A Cumberland Street
Charleston, SC 29401

Tempus books are available in France, Germany and Belgium
from the following addresses:

Tempus Publishing Group
21 Avenue de la République
37300 Joué-lès-Tours
FRANCE

Tempus Publishing Group
Gustav-Adolf-Straße 3
99084 Erfurt
GERMANY

Tempus Publishing Group
Place de L'Alma 4/5
1200 Brussels
BELGIUM

British Library Cataloguing in Publication Data.
A catalogue record for this book is available from the British Library.

ISBN 0 7524 1426-7

Typesetting and origination by Tempus Publishing.
PRINTED AND BOUND IN GREAT BRITAIN

Contents

Acknowledgements

I would like to thank the following for their help, advice, and forbearance:
Peter Kemmis Betty of Tempus Publishing Ltd.
Mrs J. Belton; Dr B. Cox, Wolfson College, Cambridge; Mr D. Dymond; Dr C. Hicks, Newnham College; Dr C. Malone, New Hall; Mrs R. Revell, Mr G. Saul, Professor J. and Mrs G. Sheail, Dr B. Short, University of Sussex.
Nigel Lutt, James Collett-White and the staff of the Bedfordshire County Record Office; Anita Hollier, Senior Archivist, B.P. Archive; Mrs E. Stazicker and the staff of the Cambridgeshire County Record Office; Christopher Jakes and the staff of the Cambridgeshire Collection; David Cleland of the East Anglian Film Archive; Dr D. Sheridan and the staff of the Mass-Observation Archive; Patrick Crouch, Haverhill Town Hall, Local History Collection; Christine Woodland, Archivist, Modern Records Centre; Richard Baxter, Mike Orchard and Andrew Perry of The Post Office Archives; the staff of the Public Records Office; Mrs M. Vaughan-Lewis and the staff of the Surrey County Record Office, University of Cambridge, Board of Continuing Education, staff and students.
Edward, Gabriel, Katie and Philip Lord who supplied accommodation, food, drink and transport as well as comments and constructive criticism.

Abbreviations

BPP – British Parliamentary Papers
BRO – Bedfordshire Record Office
CRO – Cambridgeshire Record Office
CUL – Cambridge University Library
PRO – Public Record Office
SRO – Surrey Record Office

Preface

The historian of the future will look back at the twentieth century and see it as a century of great change. At the beginning of the 1900s Britain was on the brink of discovery, but the pace of life was slow. At the end of the century life is frenetic but exotic. The discoveries made during the course of the century are both frightening and exciting. They have changed the lives of ordinary people forever.

What has this to do with the local historian? The local historian is concerned with the effects of change on the local community and the people who live in it. This book aims to help the local historian through the maze of sources available on local life in the twentieth century.

One of the problems in using twentieth-century sources is their sheer volume. No other century has produced such a mass of paperwork. Paradoxically, twentieth-century records are prone to destruction, sometimes as part of a throwaway society's policy of discarding things once used, and partly because of decay. Paper used in the first half of the century is leaching acid, and destroying what is written on it; film, photographs and tape recordings deteriorate over time. Colour photographs taken in the early 1990s are already beginning to fade, while the ephemeral nature of late twentieth-century life means that many sources exist only for the moment and are gone. The telephone conversation (unless recorded) is gone forever, the e-mail (unless printed) is lost, communication on the Internet can disappear unnoticed.

Despite these shortcomings, twentieth-century local history is exciting and accessible to everyone. No special skills are needed to read the documents, but special understanding *is* needed in order to interpret them. The following pages will interpret some of the sources, suggest where they can be found and the questions they will answer. **Colour illustration 2** is a selection of sources.

One problem of using twentieth-century sources, that the local historian should be aware of from the start, is confidentiality. Many of the sources refer to people who are still alive — or their relatives. Thus some sources are closed to public access for a number of years, or if available must be handled sensitively.

The examples in this book are drawn mainly from the areas of the country where I live or have lived, but the sources used exist for most parts of England and Wales and can be found in the Public Record Office, county record offices and local studies libraries across the country. Similarly the sources refer to the total population of England and Wales, regardless of creed, colour or gender, and the topics that have been chosen, cover areas that have most concerned society in the twentieth century. There are obvious omissions, such as employment, trade, and the decline of city centres. Unfortunately space does not permit the inclusion of these themes. They will have to be dealt with in another book.

Introduction – understanding local government

Many of the sources the local historian working on the twentieth century will be interested in using have been produced by local authorities. Thus an understanding of the different types of local authority in England and Wales, and the classes of records they have produced, is useful. Each local authority is subject to parliamentary control, and the local historian cannot ignore the interaction of politics and local government, as this may help to explain policy decisions and the records these produce.

Local government has undergone many changes in the twentieth century, but usually its records have remained in the same place — the relevant county record office. Local authority records can be divided into two main categories: records produced by the elected legislature, that is the council or its committees, and records produced by departments that put policies into practice.

County boroughs were established in 1888 and abolished in 1972. These were large towns and cities that already had a degree of freedom of control from the county in which they were situated. The 1888 County Council Act gave them complete autonomy from the county, and vested in them all the powers which the county possessed. This meant that the county borough had control over, and has left records on, education, highways, housing, markets, public health, public open spaces and police.

Between 1888 and 1972 there were 83 county boroughs in England and Wales. In 1972 county boroughs became district councils and lost control over education and housing. The records for education and housing between 1972 and 1996 will be in the county council records. However, in 1996 many county boroughs became unitary authorities and resumed their powers.

Ancient counties have been in existence since the eleventh century but administrative counties were not established until the 1888 County Council Act. This gave the county responsibility for education, health, highways, town and country planning, and roads which linked different parts of the county.

The 1972 Local Government Act created some artificial counties by altering boundaries. Notable among these were Avon in the west, and Humberside. In 1996 the components of these artificial counties reverted to their original configuration. The result of these changes is that the 1972–1996 records for these areas may be in the record office for these artificial counties, but before 1972 and after 1996 they will be in the ancient county record office.

The 1972 Local Government Act also created Metropolitan counties, which consisted of major centres of population. These include: Greater Manchester, Merseyside, South

1 Haverhill Town Council outside the Town Hall, 1911

Yorkshire, Tyne and Wear, West Midlands, and West Yorkshire. These councils created their own record offices which brought together the records of the towns and villages of their area, for example the Greater Manchester Record Office. Metropolitan counties have the same structure and responsibilities as shire counties.

Municipal boroughs were usually middling-sized towns with ancient charters which acquired municipal corporations under the 1834 Municipal Corporation Act. Municipal boroughs had responsibility for public health, housing, parks and borough roads.

In 1888 smaller towns without ancient charters became urban districts, but in 1894 this was changed and the urban district became an elected council. Urban district councils have responsibility for health, housing, cemeteries and libraries. The equivalent of the urban district council in the countryside is the rural district council.

Any parish with a population over 300 can have an elected parish council. Parishes with a population below this number have the statutory opportunity to hold parish meetings, which act as debating platforms. Parish councils have only limited powers that extend to the management of the village hall, recreation ground and allotments, but they do have the right to petition and recommend policy to the appropriate rural or urban district council. The types of records the parish council is likely to produce will include minutes of meetings, cash books, cemetery books and allotment rental books.

Two reference books which will help the local historian trace the relevant local authority are the *Municipal Yearbook* and the *Local Authorities Annual*.

1 How many people? — Births, marriages and deaths

One of the preoccupations of the local historian is how many people lived in a place, when were they born, married or died. Information on these vital events for earlier centuries can be gleaned from parish registers and the nineteenth-century census returns. For the twentieth century, although the sources that will supply this information exist, some are closed and others must be handled with care as they deal with people who still live in the community.

Many twentieth-century sources are continuations of earlier sources, while others have been created by the special demands of the time. The national census of population, which with the exception of 1941, has been taken every ten years since 1801, is a continuation. Although the enumerators' books that list individuals are closed for 100 years, the summary returns are available and can be used by local historians working on population trends. Most of these figures deal with aggregated totals, but it is possible to reconstruct the population of individual settlements. The questions that householders were asked to answer in each successive census tell the local historian about attitudes and social concerns at the time that the census was designed.

The summary returns set out, in tabular form, the results of the questions asked. The returns are divided into counties and each county constitutes a separate volume. Each volume has a list at the start giving the details of the information shown on each table, followed by a précis of the results. Every county's tables are identical and can be divided into population figures, housing, ages and condition of marriage, occupations and place of birth. A great deal of information on the local population can be extracted from the summary returns of the census.[1]

Information asked for in the census led to tables being added or subtracted from the returns. Additions in 1921 included an enumeration of orphaned children, which was an essential fact for local and national government to know, as the census was held shortly after the slaughter of the First World War. These numbers also help the local historian to estimate the social cost of the war to local society.[2] The census of 1931 included questions on those enumerated in a place as being there on census night, but only as a temporary resident. This is useful to the local historian looking at census figures for university or garrison towns.

This highlights one of the problems in using the census. It only applies to one night of the year, and the local historian has to generalise from this. Another problem is that of scale. The local historian needs to be aware of the different administrative and geographical areas being used for the tabulation of the census results. Table 2 of the county report shows that those who prepared the summary reports were aware of this problem, as it looks at the difference between ancient, administrative and registration counties. The

2 Cambridgeshire and neighbouring counties in 1911

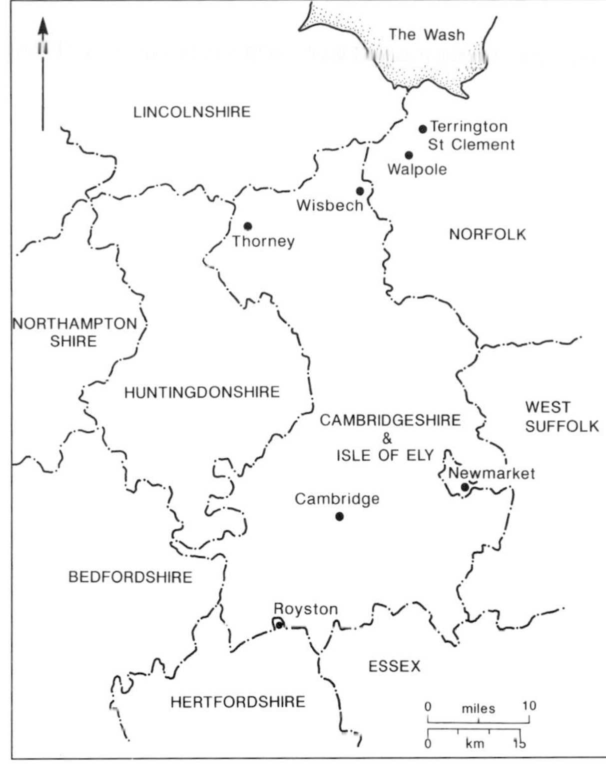

primary area that the census figures record is the registration district. These were then re-calculated for a number of other areas that include parliamentary constituencies, petty sessional divisions or civil parishes.

The difference in scale for different classes of county divisions can be illustrated from the 1901 Summary Report for Cambridgeshire.[3]

> The ancient or geographical county of Cambridgeshire was 549,723 statute acres with a population of 190,682.
> The administrative county of Cambridgeshire and the Isle of Ely was 553,219 acres with a population of 184,759.
> The registration county was 566,371 acres with a population of 200,680.

There are further complications. To arrive at the scale of the administrative county, parts of the ancient county in other administrative counties have to be deducted, in this case Norfolk, Suffolk, Essex and Huntingdonshire, and parts of ancient counties in the administrative county of Cambridgeshire have to be added. In theory this means that for Cambridgeshire, part of the ancient county at Royston was in the administrative county of Hertfordshire, and so had to be deducted from the ancient county of Cambridgeshire. However, part of the administrative county of Norfolk, and Newmarket All Saints, was in the ancient county of Cambridgeshire, while in the administrative county of West Suffolk. Conversely, parts of the registration county of Cambridgeshire were in the administrative

3 *Locations of places mentioned in the text*

counties of Hertfordshire, Huntingdonshire, and Northamptonshire, and parts of the administrative counties of Essex, Huntingdonshire, Norfolk and West Suffolk were in the registration county of Cambridgeshire (**2**).

The 1911 census report warned about the complexity of scale in the census:

> A feature by which the census in this country has always been distinguished is the variety and complexity of the areas which it has been necessary, whether for administrative reasons or for the purpose of preserving statistical continuity through changes made with but little regard to previously existing divisions, to collect and present returns. [4]

It also made an attempt to explain how the divisions were made up. Ancient or geographical counties were the basis for parliamentary divisions constituted under the 1885 Redistribution of Seats Act. Petty sessional divisions, registration, union and administrative counties were created under the 1888 Local Government Act. The boundaries usually coincide with the ancient county, but poor law unions cross parish boundaries.

The dates of these divisions are important to the local historian who is looking at a community for a period spanning the nineteenth and twentieth centuries, as it means that divisions given in the census prior to 1891 might cover a different geographical area.

The information many local historians are likely to be interested in using is that given in Tables 3, 5, 11 and 12, which deal with smaller units than the whole county. Registration

4 *Kings Mill Pond, South Nutfield*

5 *Poets' Corner Area, Jarrow, 1993. (South Tyneside Metropolitan Borough Council)*

6 *Middleton, Lancashire, town centre, c. 1925*

areas have to be aligned to parishes, and it must be remembered that the areas covered by an ecclesiastical and a civil parish are not necessarily the same. Table 14 is useful in sorting out these differences as it lists changes in civil and ecclesiastical parish boundaries. Urban historians will be interested in Tables 9, 10 and 12, which give borough returns.

The information given in Table 14 is divided into registration districts, then into sub-districts and civil parishes. The registration districts are usually based on the older local division of the hundred. This enables the local historian to match twentieth-century population trends to population in earlier centuries. Each sub-district is further divided into civil parishes.

Although these summary returns do not deal with individuals, the local historian can use them to answer many questions about the local community in the twentieth century. Linking population figures from census to census will enable the local historian to estimate population increase or decrease, and answer, at a local level, questions that historians are asking on a national scale. For example, was there massive rural depopulation in the early years of the twentieth century? Was this replaced in the latter half of the century by a move from town to country? Did the First World War result in a 'lost' generation, and what effect did this have on the local community? Can the post-war baby boom of 1947–8 be traced at a local level?

In order to illustrate comparative population trends from local communities, a number of villages, towns and cities have been chosen as a sample (**3**). These include: three Cambridgeshire villages, Linton to the east of Cambridge, Gamlingay, a large village to the west, and Nutfield (**4**), a village 25 miles from London, which is now a commuter village but was once a thriving agricultural and industrial community; three northern towns, Jarrow, where massive unemployment led to the Jarrow march in 1936 (**5**), Middleton, an old cotton town to the north of Manchester (**6**), and Whitehaven, a colliery town on the

Cumbrian coast; a garden city, Letchworth, with an advertisement promoting the new town (**col. plate 1**). A north London suburb, Hornsey, a University town, Cambridge, and an ancient city, Bath, complete the sample.

Rural depopulation occurred in Linton 1901–31, Gamlingay 1921–31, and Nutfield 1911–21 and 1961. All three of these villages show the influence of improved transport facilities on the population, with commuters from Cambridge moving out to Linton from 1951 onwards, from Cambridge and Bedford to Gamlingay in the 1960s, and from London to Nutfield in the late 1960s. Economic hardship can be seen in the decrease of population in Jarrow 1921–31, a decline which did not level out until the 1970s. Even the baby-boom years are missing from Jarrow, although they can be seen in the other settlements. Hornsey's growth is in the early twentieth century, but it slackens off later. It is easy to pinpoint the period when people started to move into Sir Ebenezer Howard's garden city at Letchworth. Cambridge shows a steady growth, Bath's population grows significantly between 1911–21 and again between 1931–51. Both of these peaks may be due to the injection into the city of personnel from the Admiralty.

The OPCS Monitor contains information about local population in the late twentieth century, while the research office of many county or city councils have brought out their own reports on local populations. In 1996 the research and information unit of Cambridgeshire County Council produced population figures which include migration figures for 1981–94, figures for births and deaths for the county and areas within it, and the city of Cambridge. The bulletins also looked at the age structure of the population with special reference to the elderly with calculations as to where pockets of pensioners were to be found.

There are other twentieth-century sources that list individuals and are open access. One of these sources is the Register of Electors. This is produced annually and contains the names and addresses of all those residents entitled to vote, males and females over the age of 18. The late twentieth-century lists should be comprehensive, but there may be some shortfall as those not wishing to be traced or taxed may avoid registration (this practice is illegal).

Electoral registers from the early twentieth century are less comprehensive. There was no universal male suffrage until 1917, and women over 30 only appear after 1918. It was not until 1927 that women over 21 were included. In the early years of the twentieth century, franchise by property qualification still existed so that electoral registers up to 1917 not only include names and addresses but also information about land holding.

Information given in the pre-1917 electoral register will include the name of the elector, the place of abode and nature of qualification to vote, which will be either a description of the property, or whether the voter is entitled to vote by virtue of being a burgess or freeman of an incorporated borough.

The electoral register will be divided into wards and electoral divisions. For example in 1908 the Cambridge Castle Ward was in Polling District 1. The register was divided into:

> Division 1 Parliamentary electors and those entitled to be enrolled as burgesses in respect of occupation.
>
> Division 2 Persons entitled in respect of the occupation aforesaid to be registered as Parliamentary electors but not to be enrolled as burgesses.

Division 3 Persons entitled in respect of the occupation aforesaid to be enrolled as burgesses, but not to be registered as parliamentary electors. This list included women, for example Eliza Allen who owned land and property in Huntingdon Road, Cambridge, Nellie Deller who owned a house on Honey Hill, and Martha Upchurch who owned a house in Castle Street.

Division 4 Persons entitled to vote as county electors, but not as parliamentary electors or as burgesses of the Borough of Cambridge.

Division 5 Persons entitled to vote at parochial elections, but not as parliamentary electors, burgesses or as county electors for the Parish of St Giles. This division also included women such as Susannah Buckstone of St Peters Street, Charlotte Gedge of Castle Street and Rebecca Pain of Pound Street.

There was also an 'old lodgers' list of persons who could claim a vote in respect of residence in a lodging. This list gives a description of the lodging. For example Thomas Maurice Juff lodged at 18 Castle Street. His furnished lodgings consisted of a sitting room on the first floor and a bedroom on the third.

Included in the early twentieth-century electoral registers were lists of persons entitled to be elected as counsellors or aldermen by virtue of their occupation, but who could not be on the electoral register. One of these was Henry Philip Chalk who lived in Linton but had an office in Alexander Street in Cambridge. The register also contained a list of freemen.

The electoral registers of the early twentieth century are more than lists of names, they are social documents in their own right, allowing the local historian to flesh out the everyday life of people like Thomas Juff.

Another source that continues through from the eighteenth and nineteenth centuries to the twentieth century, and which lists individuals, is the directory. These can be trade, town, or post office directories. These do not include the total population of a town or village, but only those with trades, and the entries are usually for the male head of household. Nevertheless the local historian can glean information about occupations, and by linking individuals through a sequence of directories, look at longevity of residence or change of occupation.

Parish registers that record baptisms, marriages and burials have been maintained in the twentieth century but only include the vital events of those who attend church, which by the late twentieth century is a minority of the local community. After the Births and Deaths Registration Act of 1836 came into operation in 1837, the only legal certification of birth, marriage or death was that obtained by the local registrar, although in the case of marriage, places of worship could be licensed to issue the appropriate certificate. Copies of these certificates are kept locally with the superintendent registrar, and centrally in the Family Records Centre, which has indexes of births, marriages and deaths in England and Wales since 1837. It also keeps indexes of legal adoptions in England and Wales since 1927 and indexes of births, marriages and deaths of British citizens abroad including deaths in the two world wars. Unfortunately these indexes are not arranged geographically but by personal name. This makes them an excellent resource for the family historian, but for local historians who want to study births, marriages and deaths in a given community, such an index is of less use. Getting closer to the vital events of the local community as a whole is likely to be difficult, but with perseverance the local historian can reconstruct the life cycle events of individuals in twentieth-century local society.

The parish register has already been mentioned as problematic in the twentieth century because of the increasing number of people who, as the century progressed, did not choose to get married or have their children baptised in church. Most people, however, are buried or cremated in the rites of their nominal faith. Burials should therefore be easier to trace and can be used as a starting point from which to examine the lives of those in the local community. The Linton burial register was analysed using parish register entries dating from 1906 to 1952.

We have to remember that the elderly were more likely to be buried with a church service and interred in the church yard, and that an increase in the number of burials may represent a rise in the population in general or the population of elderly. The figures suggest that a good proportion of the inhabitants of Linton lived to be over 70 years old. One piece of indirect evidence the burial register reveals is the change from the custom of dying at home to dying in hospital. Addenbrooks Hospital in nearby Cambridge is shown to be where some of the parishioners died from 1928 onwards. A similar pattern can be seen in Gamlingay to the west of Cambridge. In the transitional stages of the change, only infants and the middle-aged died in hospital, the elderly died in their own homes. The parish register, which reveals where the deceased died, can help the local historian to date this trend in the local community.

The information in the parish register can be related in many cases to information in the burial book maintained by the burial board. The 1853 Burial Act required each burial board to maintain a register of burials. The information included in the register will be the name of the deceased, the site of the grave within the cemetery, and the charge for the internment. This latter piece of information enables the historian to trace the changing cost of death.

The first twentieth-century entry for the Gamlingay Burial Board account book reads:

January 4th Fees for the internment of John Barford
Grave 55 sec C 2s
Sexton 3s

Charges that this board made in the early twentieth century varied and included 10s 6d for erecting a tombstone, 5s for putting a second inscription on a tombstone, and for those who wanted to reserve a grave space in advance, a charge of three guineas was made.[5] The difference in numbers when burials in the burial board book were compared with entries in the parish register showed that just over half of those interred were also entered in the parish register. This indicates that the local historian needs to be aware of alternatives to a service in the parish church. In the late twentieth century this is likely to be in the chapel of a crematorium where there should be a book of remembrance. Other sources of information on burials can be found in urban and borough council records.

Another source available on death and burial in the twentieth century are records from firms of undertakers. These may include account books, day books describing work carried out, pictures of coffins and samples of *In memoriam* cards (an unusual example of

Forth from the dark and stormy sky,
Lord, to Thine Altars shade, we fly,
Forth from the world, its hopes and fear,
Saviour, we seek Thy shelter here.

In Affectionate Memory of
Arthur William James Norcott,
Who lost his life in the R101 disaster,
on Sunday, October 5th, 1930.
Aged 29 years.

Interred in Cardington Cemetery.

7 *In memorium card for a crew member of the R101 airship, 1930. (Bedfordshire and Luton Archives and Records Service)*

such a card can be seen in **7**), plans for business premises, and if the undertaker is a limited company, annual reports of the directors.

A good example of undertakers records are those of T.H. Pacey and Son, Undertakers of Bedford, whose records cover much of the twentieth century. The information given in their account books includes the name of the deceased, date of death and sometimes age or date of birth, type and cost of coffin and lining, price of transporting the deceased to the burial place, fee for bearers, fee for the church and price for memorial cards.[6]

The price of the coffin was £7 by 1939, and the top of the range was gilded oak with electric brass, which cost £8 10s. A coffin for a stillborn baby cost 10s 6d, and tolling the church bell 1s.

This is an account of a pauper's burial for an unknown man in 1921:

> Unknown man
> Found in Stoke Brook
> Buried Sept. 29th 1921
> Parish coffin elm 10s
> Lining sides and attendants £2 14s 0d
> Carrying the body to Bletsoe 6s 6d
> 4 bearers 8s
> Church fees 11s'

'Paid' is written in red across each account including this one.

The deaths and *In memoriam* columns in local newspapers, which are available for the whole twentieth century, can tell the local historian about local customs. Local papers also contain obituaries of local worthies. Burial societies survived into the 1940s, and their records will include payments made after the death of a member. These records may be deposited with the county record office, for example the Bletsoe Burial Club records of payments on the death of members, 1900–47, can be found in the Bedfordshire Record Office.

After January 1858 probate was taken away from the church and passed to the civil probate registry. Forty of these are found in England and Wales. The original probate documents for the early twentieth century are likely to be in the local probate registry or in the county record office. Annual printed indexes up to 1935 are available at the Family Records Centre.

Information about births and marriages is also likely to be found in the local newspaper. Although these will not tell the local historian about the total population of a community the 'hatch, match, and dispatch column' can be used to look at the local seasonality of events to answer questions such as whether Easter is the preferred time for marriages, and Christmas for engagements. These columns are also useful for those local historians who are interested in naming patterns. Both the births column and the deaths column can be used, the latter by subtracting the age of the person if mentioned and looking at naming practices for that year. Thus the deaths column of the *Cambridge Evening News* 25 March 1998 revealed that in the 1900s the name Dorothy had been popular, in the 1940s the name Janet, and in 1950s the name Raymond. Of course the local historian cannot generalise from one sample but needs to keep a record from local papers over a length of time. The choice of names helps the local historian to place the local community in a wider context, and look at the influence of family, books, fashion, and the media on local life.

Babies in the latter half of the twentieth century were less likely to be christened than those born earlier who may have received a baptismal certificate (**colour plate 3**). Usually they are born in hospital rather than their mother's home, from which the hospital often lies at some distance. This is going to skew the birthplace evidence in the census returns. Local historians of the future will need to be aware of this.

Although birth certificates are available from the Family Records Centre the local historian is unlikely to want to search and pay for individual certificates, but more likely to want an overall picture of births in a locality. There are unexpected sources that give direct and indirect information on numbers of births. County council education departments needed to know how many children would be attending their schools and when. Numbers of births and the numbers of deaths of children were sent to the education authority of the county council following the 1944 Education Act, and should be found in the education authority records of the county council.

Further direct evidence of the number of births can often be found in the records of the Board of Guardians of the Poor Law. The superintendent of the workhouse was usually the registrar for the district as well and kept copies of certificates, which then passed with the rest of the Board of Guardian records into the public domain in 1948, and are now in the county record offices. Part of the Board of Guardians' records for Linton include a return of all births registered. Each infant has a number, information recorded includes when born, where born, name, sex, surname of father, or mother if unmarried, occupation of father or mother, when registered and who collected the certificate.

The information given in these registers enables the local historian to study seasonality of births in an area, the gap between birth and registration, spread of occupations and rate of illegitimacy. Once again the warning has to be given that some of those in the register and their relatives may still be in the area, so the local historian should be circumspect about mentioning names without permission.

A sample of births taken from the register for Linton for the years immediately before, during and after the First World War showed that the numbers of births rose during the

8 *A wedding couple posing in their best clothes, c.1920*

war. The rate of illegitimate births fell, but rose again after the war. Frederick and George were the most popular names for male children and Joyce for girls. Although demographic historians suggest that the seasonality of births has been flattened out by the twentieth century there was a distinct peak of births from August to October which would have meant conception from December to February. As most of the fathers' occupation details were given as 'farm labourer' this would have been in the months when work might have been slack but resources scarce. It is a pattern that needs to be investigated in other areas. Most families waited over a month before registering the child, and invariably it was the mother who collected the completed certificate.[7]

Indirect evidence for the number of births in a village can be gleaned from vaccination registers. Until 1948 the vaccination of children was the remit of the Board of Guardians of the Poor Law. Vaccination registers will, therefore, be found in records associated with the Poor Law. The vaccination register will also contain a copy of the child's birth certificate, or will give the age of an older child or adult being baptised. The vaccination register was kept in accordance with the Order of the Local Government Board 18 October 1898. The information given in the register is the name, age, residence, where the vaccination took place and details of the procedure. Information covers the whole Poor Law Union, so crosses parish boundaries.

Example from the Linton Vaccination Register:

> 1. 24th June 1915 Herbert W. Warboys, aged 6 months of Little Abington. Vaccinated in own home with NVE 9627. 4 punctures performed by W..M. Palmer. Inspected 1st July in own home, certificate issued 3rd August. Fee 6d.

Most children were vaccinated under the age of a year so the register can be a surrogate for the number of births in an area.

The adoption of children was formalised by the 1926 Adoption Act. The birth certificate of an adopted child will record this information and the Family Records Centre has an index of legal adoptions dating from 1927. Petty sessions are also involved in the adoption process but the records from the courts have a closure notice on them.

Marriages can be traced in the Family Records Centre where the index from 1912 onwards includes brides' and grooms' names. The marriage certificate itself will include the date of the event, the name of the church, chapel or registry office, the names of the partners and their civil status.

Other sources on marriages include announcements in the local paper, reports in the county magazine of the weddings of the elite, and advertisements in local papers for bridal dresses, flowers, and cars. Invitation and wedding lists can be found in family papers, and records of the courtship can be found in letters and collections of valentine cards.

None of these paper records tell the local historian how the bride felt on her great day, or what she looked like. The local historian working on the twentieth century is fortunate in having an abundance of non-documentary sources which the historian of earlier periods cannot use. Oral history is now an accepted methodology. Oral history tells the local historian about attitudes and experiences which are often absent from the written or printed document, but the local historian should be careful to try to verify information as the memory can play tricks and although there may be no intention to mislead the listener this can happen.

In 1947 the Mass Observation Survey interviewed 100 married couples on marriage. The resulting report gives some interesting statistics on attitudes to marriage including courtship, the engagement, age at marriage, sleeping arrangements and the drawbacks of being married.[8]

Photographic evidence abounds for the twentieth century, both in private homes and in public collections, local studies libraries, museums and record offices. It has been said that a picture is worth a thousand words, and that the camera does not lie. Does the posed photograph (**8**) of the wedding couple in their best clothes represent reality? Unfortunately the photographer can tell untruths, and the local historian needs to consider the photograph in its context and ask whether it shows a typical scene of its time. This is especially true of wedding photographs when everyone is in their best clothes and on their best behaviour.

Early twentieth-century films were often shot for effect rather than showing life as it was experienced. Nevertheless these give the local historian information that could never be gained from a document, such as body language and clothing. Latterly family videos will provide historians of the future valuable evidence on family life in the late twentieth century.

2 Health

The population trends discussed in the previous chapter show two important features developing in the twentieth century. One is the deliberate suppression of fertility regulating the birth rate. The other is a fall in the death rate with people living longer, so that by the late twentieth century there are likely to be fewer children in the local community, but a greater number of healthy older people and a significant number of the very old. Medical, social, and local historians have sought to explain the reason for the improvement in the death rate, and the better survival of both the elderly and robustly healthy infants. These changes have been attributed to better nutrition, better medical knowledge and health care provision, specialised research in preventative and curative medicine, better sanitation and the enforcement of compulsory legislation. The local historian is well placed to enter into these debates as local trends can enlighten national generalisations. However, the local historian may encounter a problem when looking at the health of individuals. Medical records which identify patients are closed for 100 years, and National Health Service records as opposed to those produced by local authorities are public records and come under the terms of the Public Record Act of 1958, even if these are not deposited in the Public Record Office but are kept in the county or city record office.

National records contain information on funding and application for grants, state registers of medical personnel, correspondence with local authorities on public health, approval of plans and reports on inspections. Local authority records cover the ambulance service, health centres, hospitals, nursing, infectious diseases, school health inspections and vital statistics.

Despite advances in medical science the expectation of life for the adult male was only 49 in 1911. After the National Insurance Act of that year only 40 percent of the population was insured, with only one panel doctor to every 1,777 insured patients, so that primary health care was still unavailable for a majority of the local community. Similarly, although the Maternity and Child Welfare Act of 1918 should have improved the maternal death rate it continued high and reached a peak in 1933–34 at 4.6 per 1,000 live births. It was probably the voluntary distribution of food by the National Birthday Trust that improved these figures. Local surveys may reveal the extent of the influence of voluntary schemes. Nationally, 1946 was the first year when more births were recorded in hospital than in the home. The local historian, using local records, could trace regional variations in this trend and relate these to infant and maternal mortality.

Major providers of health care in the local community were the county councils. The committee responsible for health is likely to be the Public Health and Housing Committee, which in most counties dealt with hospital services, child welfare, maternity

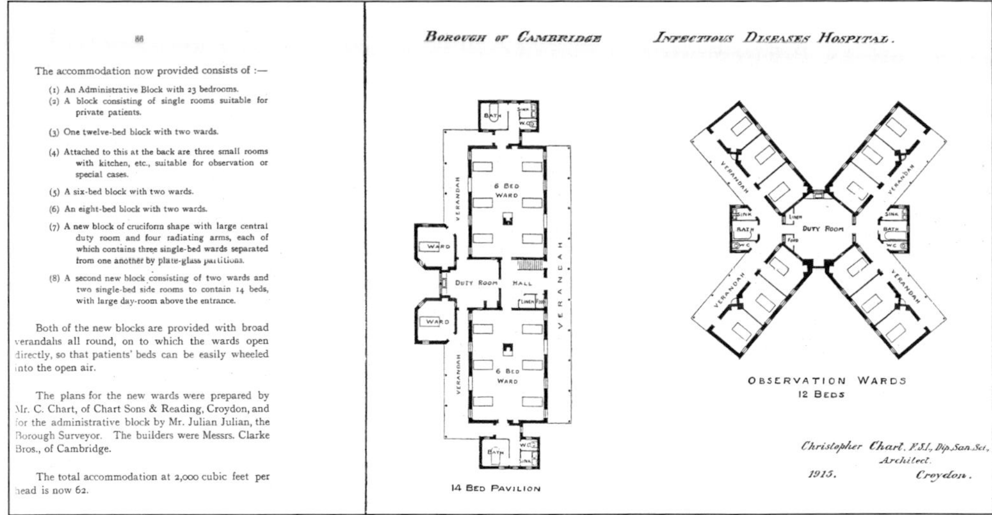

86

The accommodation now provided consists of :—

(1) An Administrative Block with 23 bedrooms.
(2) A block consisting of single rooms suitable for private patients.
(3) One twelve-bed block with two wards.
(4) Attached to this at the back are three small rooms with kitchen, etc., suitable for observation or special cases.
(5) A six-bed block with two wards.
(6) An eight-bed block with two wards.
(7) A new block of cruciform shape with large central duty room and four radiating arms, each of which contains three single-bed wards separated from one another by plate-glass partitions.
(8) A second new block consisting of two wards and two single-bed side rooms to contain 14 beds, with large day-room above the entrance.

Both of the new blocks are provided with broad verandahs all round, on to which the wards open directly, so that patients' beds can be easily wheeled into the open air.

The plans for the new wards were prepared by Mr. C. Chart, of Chart Sons & Reading, Croydon, and for the administrative block by Mr. Julian Julian, the Borough Surveyor. The builders were Messrs. Clarke Bros., of Cambridge.

The total accommodation at 2,000 cubic feet per head is now 62.

9 *Plan of the Infectious Diseases Hospital, Cambridge. (Cambridge County Record Office. By permission of Cambridge City Council)*

services and the implementation of the Midwives Act. It also dealt with public health matters such as sanitation, the inspection of nuisances, licensing of slaughterhouses, and the maintenance of a pure water supply. The committee for public health and housing usually received the report of the county medical officer, appointed members to serve on sub-committees such as the TB or milk sub-committee, and to serve on other committees such as societies for the blind or cleanliness committees.

These examples of the type of business the public health committee of a county council discussed come from the public health committee of Cambridgeshire County Council. The business included financial matters, how the services were to be funded and how much the committee would get from the county rate. It received statistics of notifiable infectious diseases from Cambridge town council and the other authorities making up the county. Figures were also received for those treated for venereal disease at Addenbrooks Hospital, which was the main provider of treatment for this in the area. It also received the annual figures for those registered blind.

These countywide figures enable the local historian to trace outbreaks of infectious diseases and relate them to other events in the county. Of especial interest to local historians working on the history of education will be those diseases associated with childhood, such as measles. These lowered attendance and in some cases caused the closure of schools.

Tuberculosis was a common disease in the first half of the twentieth century, and as it can be associated with poor nutrition and bad housing, its incidence and location give the local historian indirect evidence on the location of poverty and the local standard of living. A plan of the Cambridge Borough Infectious Diseases Hospital can be seen in figure **9**. The figures for Cambridgeshire suggest worse conditions inside Cambridge than the rural areas.

Table 1
New Cases of Tuberculosis Notified to Cambridgeshire County Council in 1943, 1946, and 1948

June 1943	County as a whole	48	Cambridge	29
April 1946	County as a whole	25	Cambridge	12
June 1948	County as a whole	45	Cambridge	25

The county ran a Tuberculosis dispensary in Cambridge with a specially trained staff and an after-care service which provided nourishment for children at risk.

Table 2
Visits to Cambridge TB Dispensary 1943, 1946 and 1948

June 1943	1173	X-rayed	773
April 1946	1564	X-rayed	450
June 1948	2209	X-rayed	1050

When the number of patients visiting the dispensary and having X-rays is compared with the number of new cases notified we can get some idea of the dread of this disease felt by the general public.

A social disease that the historian working on local morality and attitudes might wish to pursue is venereal disease. Figures for the number of patients attending the VD clinic at Addenbrooks are broken down by gender and by the type of test used and whether it was positive.

Table 3
Visits to Addenbrooks Hospital VD Clinic 1943, 1946, 1948

	Tested	Positive	Male	Female
June 1943	582	120	74	56
April 1946	714	157	95	62
June 1948	630	125	97	28

Again the difference between the number tested and the number found positive indicates to the local historian the scope of the fear of having VD, and that other genito-urinary infections were thought by the sufferer to be symptoms of VD. These figures could be an indirect but quantifiable measurement on morality and social attitudes.

The county council relied on the county medical officer of health to collect and collate information from across the county and report it to the Public Health Committee. As well as including direct evidence on disease, the county medical officer also reported on the monthly rainfall and the state of the county's water supply. The county medical officer also made suggestions on policy. In 1910 the county medical officer of health for Cambridgeshire drew up a handbill to inform households about sanitary methods for the disposal of domestic refuse and the prevention of food pollution. In the same year he had to close seven schools due to a severe outbreak of whooping cough, and he also reported on, and suggested improvements to, the isolation hospitals in the county.

Cambridge itself was a county borough with its own public health committee. The general minutes of this body cover a wide range of subjects. On 24 November 1936 matters covered included the submission of the sanitary inspector's daily journals, the issue of slaughterhouse licenses, reports on isolation hospitals, common lodging houses, the water supply and the public analysts report on samples of food and drink taken randomly from suppliers. The general committee received a report from the Maternity and Child Welfare Committee on the winter visits of school health visitors, and it agreed that it would send patients to the Ely Diocesan Maternity Home at a cost of 10s per patient.

In the same year Cambridge had to implement the Midwives Act, when it became the duty of every authority to secure whole-time, and a sufficient number of salaried midwives to attend women in their own homes. Two midwives were appointed in Cambridge at salaries of £200–300. Patients were to pay fees on a sliding scale based on income, while milk, virol, and cod liver oil were to be supplied for mother and child by the council.

In 1937 the Maternity and Child Welfare Committee set up an 'interested bodies' sub-committee. This included the Cambridgeshire County Council Insurance Committee, the Voluntary Association for Maternity and Child Welfare, the Friendly Societies Council, the Cambridge and District Branch of the National Council for Women, the local division of the British Medical Association and the local branch of the Women's Co-operative Guild. This list opens up a number of other possibilities for the local historian to explore, and extends the debate on the voluntary provision of healthcare into one which was not divided between public and voluntary but was based on co-operation. The records of the voluntary organisations may be in the county record office, or if it still exists in the headquarters of the organisation.[1]

The council was also concerned with inspecting and condemning houses that were unfit for human habitation. The sanitary inspector took charge of the fumigation of houses after an outbreak of infectious disease and by the 1930s part of the council's responsibility extended to the provision and maintenance of public hot baths and conveniences, dustbins and the sanitation of caravan sites. In November of every year between 1933–9 each council had to play its part in National Rat Week. This was preceded by a notice placed in the local newspaper which recorded the number of rats killed in the previous year as a target to beat.

District and borough councils were also involved in health education. In conjunction with the National Council for Health Education, health exhibitions were arranged, details of which can be found in council minutes and local newspapers. A health exhibition held in the Guildhall in Cambridge during September 1938 included lectures on such subjects as 'Heredity in Man', 'Sleep', and 'Air Raid Precautions'. The exhibition was attended by 7,683 people, and there is some indirect evidence of disagreement between the national and borough councils as the national council wanted to charge a 3d admission fee but the local council refused to do this.[2]

Special reports found in council records could contain reports on the sanitary conditions in the area. These reports, peculiar to each council, may include the number of births registered, the causes and seasonality of deaths, and poor law statistics, including the number of vagrants receiving relief. Council records should also include reports from

15

DENTAL CARD (FRONT).

Cambridge Dental Institute for Children.

12a, PARKSIDE.

Hours :

9 a.m. to 1 p.m. 2.30 p.m. to 5 p.m.
Thursday and Saturday—9 a.m. to 1 p.m.

Name.. *Age*......................

Address ....

....

To come on

Monday ....1908, at ....o'clock.
Tuesday................................ " " .... "
Wednesday .... " " .... "
Thursday .... " " .... "
Friday .... " " .... "
Saturday .... " " .... "

PLEASE BE PUNCTUAL.

PLEASE BRING THIS CARD AT EACH VISIT.

P.T.O.

DENTAL CARD (BACK).

How to take Care of the Teeth.

1. **The teeth must be kept clean.**
2. **Use a small tooth brush with stiff bristles ; use a little soap and some prepared chalk.**
3. **Brush all the teeth thoroughly, especially the back ones. Brush all surfaces of the teeth.**
4. **Clean the teeth immediately before going to bed. Take no food of any sort afterwards. Clean the Teeth again in the morning.**

CLEAN TEETH DO NOT DECAY.

10 'How to take care of your teeth', dental card from Borough of Cambridge Medical Officers Report, 1909. (Cambridge County Record Office. By permission of Cambridge City Council)

health visitors giving information about the care of infants. These date from 1906. The figures for the Health Visitors Reports for the Borough of Cambridge 1906–12 show conclusively that 'breast is best'.

Table 4
Percentage of infant deaths showing feeding method Cambridge 1906–12

Breast fed only	2.5
Mixed	6.5
Cows' milk	7.0
Condensed milk	10.0
Other	7.0

In the 1913 report there is evidence that the council were trying to educate mothers in better hygiene though 'Mothers Schools'.[3]

The School Dental Service reports, and the reports of the school medical inspectors give a sorry picture of child health in Cambridge in the second decade of the twentieth century. The school dental inspector suggested that the damage was done to the children's teeth by the time they were 11, and a notice was sent to parents 'Clean Teeth do Not Decay' (**10**). The school medical inspector found 'underfed children, some very thin'. The average weight for boys aged ten was 3st 10lb and their average height was 3ft 11in. When compared with other figures for the same period we find that boys attending Christ's Hospital School, at the same age, were likely to be on average 6in taller and at least 5lb heavier. By comparing other areas the local historian can begin to identify those regions where children were less well nourished and were not developing as they should.[4]

In the late twentieth century there has been an increasing tendency to take the provision of healthcare out of the hands of the smaller authorities and vest this in larger regional bodies. From 1947–74 this was either the National Health Service Executive Council or the Regional Health Board, and in 1974–82, area health authorities. The minutes and accounts of these bodies are in the public domain, available for the local historian to use in the reference library of a town or city, or the local studies library. An example of the topics covered by these can be judged from the minutes of the East Anglian Regional Health Authority for 19 April 1974. The subjects under discussion included revenue allocation and other financial matters, reports from the committee on conditions in psychiatric and long stay hospitals, the Regional Scientific Committee, and the Suffolk Dental Advisory Committee. The provision of a casualty service at Thetford Cottage Hospital was discussed, and there were reports from community health councils.

Owing to the confidential nature of many medical records, part of the proceedings were 'in camera' or closed access. However, the proceedings of the 'open' meetings of the health authorities of the 1980s and 1990s are available. An examination of the topics discussed in the 1990s shows a change in the concerns of regional health authorities. On 23 February 1994 the open session of the East Anglian Regional Health Authority received the report of the regional general manager, which discussed financial matters and received reports on disability and rehabilitation services in the region, and reports on multiple sclerosis, hearing impairment and asthma. An item which would not have been on the agenda in the 1970s was applications for GP fund-holding schemes. Other topics show an increased concern for efficiency through comparisons with other regions. Comparisons across the region on the waiting time for in-patients to get a bed, the time taken to see out-patients or accident and emergency cases, the number of patients whose operations were cancelled at least twice and the time taken for an ambulance to arrive at an emergency add an element of competition into health care, which may be to the benefit of the patient. The meeting also discussed the provisions of the 'Patients Charter' and how the region would implement these, which shows a new measure of accountability towards the client.

When using regional health records the local historian must be aware of the geographical area these cover, and changes in this. Changes in the organisational aspects of health care are mostly due to government policy, and it is from central government that the local health authority gets its funding. The Ministry of Health was created in 1919

11 *Staff outside Kedington (Suffolk) Union Workhouse Infirmary. (Haverhill Local History Collection)*

when responsibility for health was transferred to it from the Local Government Board of Health.

Ministry of Health records at the PRO are found in class MH. MH 30 is the county register which includes the annual reports of the county medical officer of health for the early years of the century. MH 31/8 and MH 48 are county files of correspondence between the ministry and councils. Of special interest to the local historian will be MH 66, which are the reports of local health provisions taken in 1936–7.

MH 66/1 is the survey for Bedfordshire. The report starts with a description of the county, resources and population. Mortality statistics are compared with the national average. Names of the medical staff employed by the county are given with a judgement on their performance, types of hospitals, numbers of beds. The survey included county and municipal boroughs which had additional information on housing, water supply, sewage disposal, and the inspection of food. MH 66/823, the survey for Poole, shows that although the town had a sewage works it was discharging waste into the sea at Branksome Chine. Despite this the town had a death rate of 11.71 per 1,000 which was just below the national average of 11.8.[5] Other sources in the PRO of direct interest to the local historian are MH 67 Joint Hospital Board Reports and MH 69 Executive Committee Reports, which include correspondence with GPs. The health services funded by central government and administered by local authorities cannot operate without the providers and carers. Providers can be divided into hospital and neighbourhood providers, the latter being the GP's surgery, health centre and local clinic.

Hospitals can be divided into categories in two different ways. One way is to divide them with reference to the main funding body; the other is to divide them by function.

12 *Dalrymple House, Home for Inebriates, Rickmansworth, Hertfordshire. (Mr G. Saul)*

For most of the twentieth century, hospitals have been funded either by voluntary donations — known as voluntary hospitals, public funds known as public hospitals, or by fees charged to the patient, i.e. private hospitals. After the creation of the National Health Service many voluntary hospitals became part of the nationally funded hospital service. Public hospitals grew out of the Poor Law Infirmaries, which were separated from the workhouse in 1914, given their own regulations and administered by a medical superintendent. The staff of one such hospital can be seen in figure **11**. From 1900–14 the hospital records will be with the records of the Poor Law Guardians, and from 1914–29 either filed with the poor law records or found under the medical superintendents' records. The Board of Guardians was abolished in 1929 and in 1930 local authorities took over the responsibility for the Poor Law Hospitals, and the records from 1930 will be with the appropriate council's records. Union infirmary records may include admissions, records of drugs dispensed, and reports from the medical superintendent. Records from after the abolition of the poor law will include minutes of committees, ledgers, admission and discharge books, daily log books, correspondence, inventories of furniture and other property. These records are subject to a 100-year closure for any which refer to individual patients.

A way of finding what types of institutions existed in an area in the first half of the twentieth century is to use tables 16 and 17 of the summary report of the Census of Population for 1911. Table 16 lists all workhouse establishments, lunatic asylums, prisons, hospitals, certified reformatories, and industrial schools, and inebriate retreats county by county giving the number of inmates divided by sex, and the number of staff and their

13 Children's Ward, Bedford County Hospital, c.1900. (Bedfordshire and Luton Archives Records Service)

families present on census night. Table 17 gives the addresses of the institutions. For example from these tables we find two inebriate retreats in Hertfordshire, one at Dalyrymple House in Rickmansworth (**12**) that had 17 inmates, and the other Buntingford House at Aspeden with 13 inmates. Not every county had such a retreat and some counties financed regional retreats such as the East Counties Inebriate Reformatory at Kenninghall in Norfolk, which had 258 inmates and a staff of 27.

Other reference tools that the local historian could use in order to trace hospitals are H.C. Burdett (ed.) *Burdett's Hospitals Annual and Yearbook of Philanthropy*, which covers the years 1900–24, and the Central Bureau of Hospital Information's *The Hospital's Yearbook* which starts in 1900.

Local hospital records will be in borough and county council records and are classified as 'public records'. These are subject to closure, as directed by the Public Records Act, of 100 years for any record from which it is possible to identify an individual, 75 years for sensitive material relating to children, and 30 years for other sensitive material such as disciplinary proceedings, complaints, or nurses' performance. Hospitals have been given the right to hold the records for 30 years after creation before depositing these with a place of safe deposit, usually the county record office.[6]

The type of material available for the local historian to use will include hospital committee minutes and the minutes of the committee of visitors (a voluntary inspectorate), financial records showing expenditure, salaries and wages, property deeds, details of maintenance and plans of buildings, and proposals for development. Special hospitals often had farms or industrial complexes attached, and as well as allowing the local historian to look at the activities of the hospital, the records pertaining to these contain much indirect evidence on prices, wages, and farming practices. The records of Fairfield Hospital in Bedfordshire are a good example of this. These include the bailiff's cash books, brewing accounts, stock books and information on agricultural wages.[7]

Hospitals usually produce a printed annual report. Information contained in these will vary depending on the hospital, but an excellent example is the Annual Report of the Bedford County Hospital for 1947. An early photograph of the children's ward is shown in figure **13**. This report includes a list of hospital administrators, medical and nursing staff. The figures for the numbers of beds available are given and compared with the figures for the previous year, and are broken down into general, maternity and private. Figures are given for the number of patients treated and the number of deaths, the number of out-patients, the average stay in the ward of in-patients, and the average cost per week per patient. The report includes news about appointments, lists of governors and benefactors (this was a voluntary hospital), donations from fundraising and how this was achieved, and an account sheet. The report concludes with a geographical analysis of the patients treated.[8] Any local historian interested in the centrality of a county town would find the geographical analysis of patients an important source. Comparison with other hospitals will show whether the way in which the Bedford County Hospital treated its patients was typical. Changes in attitudes to treatment over time can also be shown.

Table 5 Average Length of Stay in Hospitals of In-Patients, in days [9]

	1911	**1921**	**1938**	**1946**	**1947**
Cambridge Addenbrooks	26.5	25.8	17.8		
All General Hospitals	25.6	23.8	17.3		
St Bartholomew's, London	26.5	23.8	19.4		
Oxford, Radcliffe	21.0	25.8	16.2		
Bedford General				15.82	16.17
Bedford Maternity					11.64

In view of the fact that the late twentieth-century patient stay in hospital is likely to be only one or two days, the local historian will be interested in the effects of this change and whether this is the result of better treatment, a change in attitudes to hospitalisation, financial considerations, or better conditions in the home (meaning that the patient can return to a warm and hygienic environment).

Hospital minutes will shed light on the activities of doctors, nurses and auxiliary members of the hospitals. For example from the minutes of the Biggleswade Joint Hospitals Committee for 1946 we learn that the ambulance driver had to combine his duties with being general maintenance man for the hospital, and that he had a tied house in the hospital grounds. The same minutes show that there was a quick turnover of senior nursing staff at the hospital, and that relations between them were not always of the most cordial.[10] Locations of places in Bedfordshire mentioned in the text can be seen in figure **14**.

Of especial interest to the local historian will be neighbourhood nursing care. Much community nursing was the result of voluntary endeavour such as the Nursing

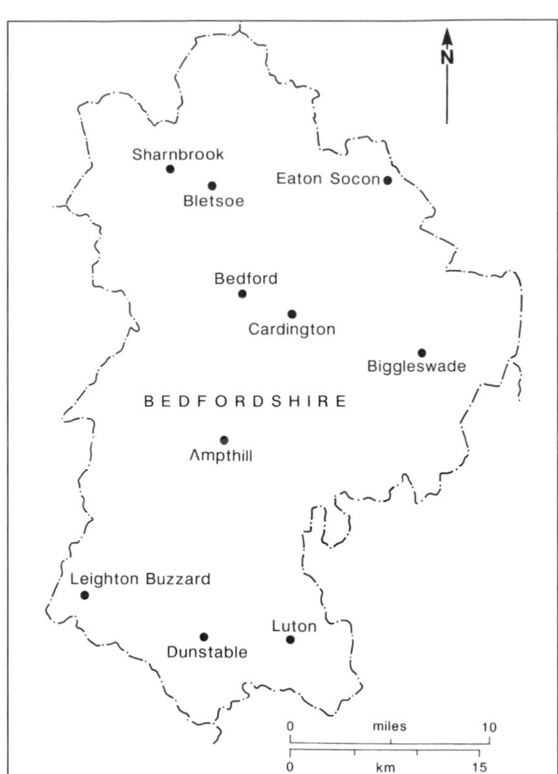

14 *Locations of places in Bedfordshire mentioned in the text*

Association, which through its local branches provided a district nurse service in rural areas to those who subscribed to the association. The branch records should be found in the county record office. A branch was formed in Cardington in Bedfordshire by 1900, when the first minutes appear. The association employed a nurse on a three-year contract with a salary of 14s a week. The nurse was responsible for the upkeep of the association's bicycle and was allowed to go out without leave for one hour at a time when there was opportunity. The new nurse employed in 1905 had to sign an agreement that she would keep the bicycle in good repair in every way, except the tyres. But the minutes record that the committee had to reprimand her for not starting the day at 9a.m. or staying on duty until 8 in the evening, and not leaving word with a neighbour when she was going out.

In 1910 the salary was raised to 19s a week, but the bicycle was in such bad repair the association sold it for 5s. At this time the nurse was awarded three weeks holiday, which was increased to four weeks in 1912. In 1918 a new bicycle was purchased and the nurse was given a bicycle allowance of £2 per annum. Her salary was 34s 6d a week by that time and her responsibilities were increasing. She had to attend disabled soldiers and her area was increased to include the village of Shortstown, built by Short Brothers for their aircraft workers. The result was that a second nurse had to be employed. The senior nurse received 52s a week and the junior 42s. In March 1931 there were 212 subscribers to the association, and in that year the nurses made 1,714 visits.[11]

Another branch of the nursing profession is midwifery, the status of which was considerably improved after the Midwives Acts of the early twentieth century. In order to

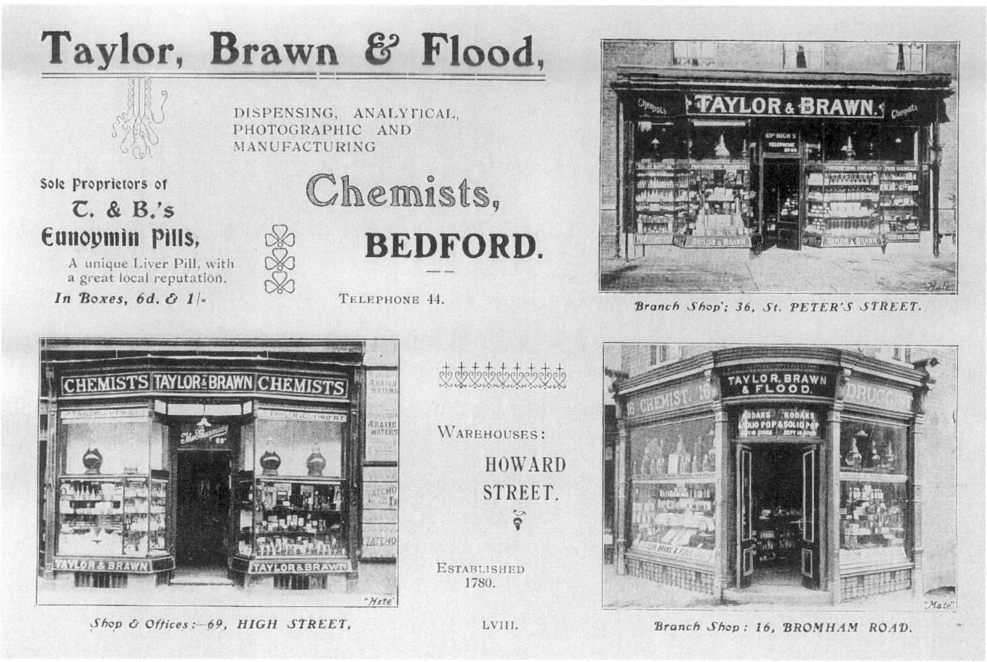

15 *Advertisement for Taylor, Brawn and Flood, chemists, Bedford. (Bedfordshire and Luton Archives Records Service)*

further improve their position county associations of midwives were formed. One of the earliest was the Bedfordshire Association of Midwives, which held its first meeting in the Shire Hall in 1912. The county midwives associations aimed to educate members and improve their efficiency. They also agreed on the prices that should be charged for confinements. This was to be on a sliding scale between 10s 6d and 15s, depending on circumstances. To improve their education a series of lectures was held, given by doctors and other professionals. Also interleaved with the minutes of the Bedfordshire Association was a report of a conference held in November 1925 by the National Council for the Unmarried Mother and her Child, of which the subject was infant mortality. Although the midwives were recognised as trained medical practitioners it was felt that their professional standing would be enhanced with a salaried professional service, and the Bedfordshire Association suggested that it should lead the way in this.[12]

Under the Pharmacy and Poisons Act of 1933 local commercial pharmacies were required to register with the appropriate local authority. Both the list of those applying to be registered and the list of those placed on the register should help the local historian to trace local chemists, while information on the duties and hours of opening will also be found in council records. Similarly dentists were also required to register with the local health authority, and these registers will help the local historian to reconstruct the dental health of the local community. Nursing homes were also registered.

The records of commercial chemists may have been deposited with the county record office, for example the records of the firm of Messrs Taylor, Brown and Flood Chemists of Bedford, which date from 1900–37 (**15**), or those of H. Flanders of Mill Road Cambridge, pharmacist and dispensing opticians, whose records cover the period 1880–1962. These records include prescription books, records of eye tests, daybooks and ledgers.[13] Records covering doctors practices and surgeries will either be closed or in private hands.

The other element of health care in the local community that the local historian should not forget is that provided by organisations that rely on voluntary help and subscriptions. These organisations either provide administrative support for professionals, or employ their own staff to give primary health care, such as in the case of the Macmillan Nurses. Two long-established voluntary organisations involved in health care are the St Johns Ambulance Brigade and the Red Cross, which exist to train amateurs. Some local branch records for these have been deposited in the county record or local studies library, but in the case of the Red Cross, county branch records from 1909 onwards are at the Training Centre in Surrey.

Sub-branch records exist locally, as in the case of the Chippenham Division of the Cambridgeshire Red Cross, which met in 1914 to take an inventory of its property. This included bell tents, baskets with straps, lockers, pegs and ropes for beds and a 'complete set of books and forms for field days and mobilisation'. Brandy and bandages were among their medical stores, and the Church of England School at Cheveley and the cricket pavilion had been earmarked as hospitals. The description of these records the exact measurements, so this is evidence for the local historian looking either at local schools or local sports facilities.[14] A useful reference book for tracing local branches of charitable organisations is the *Charities Yearbook*.

The local historian will also find contemporary medical records at the Wellcome Institute. These include the local branch material for the Family Planning Association and the papers of the Association of County Medical Officers of Health 1902–74. The records of the British Medical Association are held in their headquarters, as are those of the Royal College of Nursing, while the records of the Confederation of Health Service Employees (COHSE) are in the Modern Records Centre of the University of Warwick.

Although the local historian will need to sift through the multiplicity of official and voluntary bodies concerned with health in the local community, the sources available should enable the local historian to trace the development of healthcare at a local level and relate this to advances in medical science and changes in attitudes of the medical profession and local society. The wealth of indirect evidence contained in these sources also makes them valuable for other areas of inquiry, especially areas directly related to good health such as quality housing.

3 Housing

The importance of good quality housing for the health of the nation did not escape the notice of national and local government. The inferior nature of much of Britain's housing came to light during the First World War. Its exposure led to a campaign to provide 'Homes for Heroes'; slum clearance and the provision of council housing followed.

Working-class housing, however, is only one strand in the skein of local housing provision. Types of housing help to determine the character of an area. A 1960s' concrete jungle of high-rise flats has blighted many urban areas, while private housing estates grafted onto rural villages have altered the structure of whole communities. Furthermore, fluctuations in house prices give the local historian an insight into the economics of the local community.

The concern of central government about the nation's housing stock is revealed in the questions asked in the national census. From the nineteenth century householders had been asked for information about the numbers of houses inhabited or uninhabited in an area, and the numbers being built at the time of the census. Tables 19-21 from the 1901 census onwards deal specifically with the number of tenements, rooms available, and how these were occupied, with the figures being broken down into combinations that include the administrative county, county boroughs, municipal, urban and rural districts respectively. But what was a house or tenement? The compilers of the 1911 census admitted that it was difficult to define these, and the classification of houses has baffled census administrators. From 1851–1901 a house was 'all that space with external and party walls of a property'. In 1911 houses were deemed to include:[1]

(a) ordinary dwelling houses and dwellings above shops
(b) houses connected for the occupation of two or more families
(c) maisonettes or double houses
(d) blocks of flats or model dwellings, each block reckoned as being one house irrespective of distinct suites of rooms
(e) blocks of shops with residences above
(f) hotels, clubs and boarding houses
(g) institutions such as workhouses, hospitals and asylums
(h) offices, warehouses, and business establishments with resident caretakers

This definition offers great scope for ambiguity, and further ambiguity occurred in the instructions to enumerators who were to regard a dwelling or tenement as 'a place in which any person entitled to receive a schedule usually lives'.[2] The 1911 census produced tables of house sizes estimated as per 1,000 per population.

Table 6 Counties with the highest and lowest number of houses with less than 4 rooms, per 1,000 population, from the 1911 Census

Highest		Lowest	
Northumberland	559	Soke of Peterborough	74
London	541	Bedfordshire	80
Durham	506	Isle of Wight	80

Table 7 Counties with the highest and lowest number of families with less than 4 persons per family given as per 1,000 families, from the 1911 census[3]

Highest		Lowest	
Cardiganshire	530	Glamorgan	295
Anglesey	483	Monmouth	311
Cambridgeshire	471	Durham	326
Isle of Wight	471	Staffordshire	349

The national average family size was 4.77. Industrial areas had larger families or households, agricultural counties smaller, which was part of the rural depopulation process. For example, young adults moved from Cardiganshire and Anglesey to swell the population of Glamorgan and Monmouth, working in the coal mines and steel works.

In 1921 the tenement was redefined as a 'structural separate building'. This was to include flats. The summary figures for 1921 show less overcrowding and smaller average family size. In Cambridgeshire the average family size in 1911 was 4.06 which had fallen to 3.86 in 1921. Similar trends can be observed in other counties. The 1921 census reveals, however, that overcrowding is increasing in rural areas with higher room occupancy in rural districts such as Ramsey and Thorney in Cambridgeshire, than in the borough itself.[4]

By the time the 1951 census was taken the compilers were not so much concerned with housing shortages, but with the lack of amenities. Questions asked whether the household had exclusive use of cold and hot water taps, baths and WC's. A question asked in 1961 was whether the house was permanent or moveable, and how many rooms it had.

Table 8 Permanent Dwellings as a percentage of all houses for a sample of counties 1961

Durham	95.2
Derbyshire	95.2
Staffordshire	92.9
Suffolk, East	92.5
Suffolk, West	92.0
Surrey	85.8
Devon	85.4

The lower numbers of permanent houses in Devon and Surrey reflect the high numbers of caravans and chalets in Devon and the existence of several large gypsy encampments, mobile home parks, and the survival into the 1960s of pre-fabs.

Table 9 Houses with less than 4 rooms as a percentage of all houses, for a sample of counties, 1961 [5]

Surrey	21.6
Devon	24.7
Suffolk, East	29.4
Derbyshire	31.2
Suffolk, West	36.4
Staffordshire	39.1
Durham	55.3

This reverses the trend on the preceding table, and shows that although there might be more temporary homes in Devon and Surrey, the rest of the housing stock was of acceptable size. Much of that in Durham, however, was still small and shows little improvement in the 50 years that had passed from 1911.

By comparing across censuses the local historian can look at improvements in the quality of life.

Table 10 Lack of Amenities in a Sample of Counties given as a percentage of all household 1961 and 1971

	Derbyshire		**Devon**		**Surrey**	
	1961	**1971**	**1961**	**1971**	**1961**	**1971**
No hot water	19.2	6.3	21.9	6.1	12.8	3.3
No fixed bath	24.9	11.0	19.2	7.4	10.5	4.1
No inside WC	11.1	1.7	6.0	1.1	2.1	0.8

In the decade between 1961 and 1971 there had been major improvements in household amenities in these and other counties. The 1991 census sought to distinguish between home ownership and the rented sector, and in the rented sector between houses rented from the local council and those rented from private landlords.

Table 11 Results from the 1991 census for a sample of counties on home ownership and other amenities[6] (given as a percentage, except for last statistic)

	Cambs	**Derbys**	**Devon**	**Durham**	**Staffs**	**Surrey**
Owned	65.2	71.4	72.5	62.4	73.1	77.4
Private Rental	15.8	9.4	14.6	8.7	8.0	10.5
Council Rental	19.0	19.2	12.9	28.9	18.9	12.1
No bath	1.0	1.0	1.4	0.7	1.1	1.1
No car	24.8	31.3	27.3	39.7	28.2	17.8
Persons per rm.	1.4	1.4	1.5	1.6	1.7	1.4

Local historians will observe trends in this table that will lead to more detailed studies. For example, higher council house occupancy would appear to result in better household amenities but overall a less wealthy population with low car ownership. Another government publication which gives information on urban housing is the 1978 National

Dwelling and Housing Survey which investigated housing provision covering regional patterns, boroughs and districts (districts being larger housing areas, for example Sunderland, Bristol or Sandwell). The survey was published by HMSO and can be found in reference libraries. It looked at the number of dwellings, number of households and whether these were in multiple dwellings, the number of married couples and the number of lone parents. The statistical analysis of the latter was a new departure. The survey estimated the number of dwellings surplus to demand. In London this was only 0.4 percent but in rural Suffolk in 1978 there were 3.2 percent surplus houses. Average rateable values are compared, as are household amenities, types and size of houses, and the socio-economic group of the occupants.

Table 12 Comparison of types of houses in county boroughs in 1978 in percentages

	Most		**Least**	
Detached	Dudley	16.1	Manchester	2.5
Semi	Wakefield	46.3	Liverpool	19.4
Terraced	Liverpool	48.2	Dudley	15.8
Flats	Gateshead	21.9	Wakefield	6.3

This table tells the local historian about the character of an area through its housing stock. Dudley in the West Midlands has large detached houses and few terraces. It is possible, however, that the detached houses at Dudley were in multiple occupation. Other information in the survey reveals that these houses, which had on average four bedrooms, were home to small households. Other tables in the survey cover basic amenities and length of occupation. Over half of Dudley's residents had lived there for more than 10 years, which at 53 per cent was more than any other town in the survey.

Part 2 of the survey covered the shire counties.

Table 13 Comparison of types of Houses in Shire Counties in 1978 in percentages

	Most		**Least**	
Detached	Dorset	40.3	Durham	9.1
Semi	Staffordshire	43.9	Cornwall	18.2
Terraced	Durham	47.7	Dorset	14.4

The correlation between a low number of detached houses and a high number of terraced is obvious, and highlights long-term trends that can be observed in county Durham from the early years of the twentieth century. At this time 44.1 percent of Durham's entire housing stock was council housing. The survey indicates that the smallest households were found in East Sussex and that Cornwall was the county with least household amenities but the largest retired population.

Part 3 of the survey repeats the process for metropolitan districts.

16 Council houses, Haverhill. (Haverhill Local History Collection)

Table 14 Comparison of types of houses in metropolitan districts, 1978 in percentages

	Most		Least	
Detached	Solihull	21.5	St. Helens	8.00
Semi	Barnsley	49.9	Calderdale	33.9
Terraced	Coventry	53.5	Solihull	17.9

Once more we see the correlation between more detached and less terraced types of housing, and throughout subsequent tables in the survey, Solihull is shown to have larger houses with more amenities than those in other metropolitan districts. However, although the houses in Solihull were likely to be owner-occupied, the owner was paying for these through a mortgage. In Calderdale where 58.3 percent of houses had no central heating the houses were owned outright.

The final part of the survey covered non-metropolitan districts.

Table 15 Comparison of types of houses in non-metropolitan districts, 1978 in percentages[7]

	Most		Least	
Detached	S. Holland	51.8	Hull	1.8
Semi	Epsm./Ewell	40.1	Hull	13.9
Terraced	Hull	67.7	S. Holland	8.9

Epsom and Ewell were shown to have smaller households and more amenities than elsewhere, for example whereas 99 percent of households in Epsom had their own hot water supply, 5 percent in Plymouth had no access to hot water. Although the 1978 survey does not cover individual villages, it does enable the local historian to build up a picture of housing stock in different regions, and of the socio-economic character of an area.

The annual report of the Ministry of Health, which took over responsibility for housing and slum clearance after the 1919 Addison Housing Act, helps the local historian to trace the progress of council house provision. The report gives the building figures for each local authority as well as the figures for the numbers of private houses built. In 1930 the figures for Jarrow, Middleton and Whitehaven show that the local authorities were building the biggest share of new houses, whereas in Bath, Cambridge and Letchworth more private houses were being built. Throughout the 1930s the biggest providers of council houses were Birmingham, Leeds, Liverpool and Sheffield. A compilation of figures produced by the Ministry of Housing and Local Government in 1966 shows that the situation changed after the Second World War. A typical example of a council house is shown in figure **16**.

Table 16 Houses completed 1945–66 for a sample of towns[8]

	Council Houses	Private Houses	Total
Bath	3624	3615	7239
Cambridge	6059	3536	9595
Jarrow	384	269	4111
Letchworth	2492	973	3465
Middleton	2246	2216	4462
Whitehaven	3089	596	3685

The difference in total houses built shows the relocation of the economic centre of the country, away from the heavy industrial areas of the north to the light technological industries of the south.

The increasing control of central government over the activities of local authorities means that for many local records on housing, the other half of the story can be found in state records. For the early twentieth century these are in PRO class HLG or Housing and Local Government. HLG 14 deals with the sanction of loans for developments. The class is arranged under the name of the local authority and the information given includes the amount sanctioned, the period of the loan and its purpose, which will include a description of the site. HLG 49 contains submissions and approvals of housing developments. HLG 49/260 is the correspondence and approval for Letchworth Urban District Council to build 186 houses at Hillbrow in Letchworth in 1924. A total of 110 of the houses were to be the parlour type of houses and 76 non-parlour. The details given about the houses extend to the number of hooks to be placed in storage cupboards, and the type of garden gate to be provided.

The applications also contain an amount of indirect evidence that will be of interest to the local historian. A list of loans outstanding show that Letchworth council had spent

£25,516 14s 6d on street improvements, £5,166 16s 7d on a pleasure ground and £807 7s 5d on a public convenience. The file for Letchworth shows that a loan of £4,000 was sanctioned and tenders to build the houses were sought in December 1924.[9]

Other classes in the PRO that the local historian working on housing may be interested in are HLG 4 and 5 which cover details of planning schemes from 1905–51, and HLG 24 files on re-housing schemes with plans and maps.

One response of the government to housing shortages was to designate areas as new towns. HLG 90 deals with new towns, the progress of works, complaints and objections. HLG 129 contains planning inspectorate appeals, and HLG 132 the decision taken and copies of letters.

At county level the county council was less likely to be involved in building houses than the district authorities. However, county councils have responsibility for co-ordinating housing with town and country planning. Evidence of the deliberations on these will be in the minutes of the appropriate committee, housing and town and country planning committees. City, county borough, urban and rural districts councils were more intimately involved with housing at a local level. This involvement not only covered building council houses, but in giving planning permission for new houses and additions and alterations to old, keeping a register of property sales, and when local taxes were assessed on property in assessing property values and compiling rate books. All of these functions produced records that the local historian working on housing will be able to use.

Housing committee minutes record discussion on proposals for council housing and the consideration of tenders. The abstract discussions can be related to the more concrete documents and plans, tenancy agreements, rents and rate books. These, with the records in the PRO allow the local historian to reconstruct the development of a type of housing which is peculiar to the twentieth century — local authority housing.

An example of the use of these documents comes from Ampthill in Bedfordshire. The minutes of the Housing Committee of Ampthill UDC show that on 6 September 1927 the committee discussed 'the question of the erection of homes for the working classes . . .'. On 1 December the council decided to buy one acre of land in Olive Street and build eight houses. The owner of the land in Olive Street refused to sell it, but on 12 February 1928 the Duke of Bedford intervened and agreed to sell the council land for building in Station Road. The council then had to apply to the ministry for a subsidy — details of the application, plans, sanctions and correspondence are in the PRO and are a good illustration of the fusion of local and national records in the twentieth century. The council received permission to build, and the subsidy in June 1928 and the work was placed out to tender. In November 1928 a notice was displayed in the town inviting applications for tenancies from the public, and by 22 December 22 applications had been received for the eight houses, and a shortlist was drawn up by the Housing Committee. This is evidence of a demand for good quality houses let at an economic rent, in this case 6s 9d a week. The complex was called 'The Crescent' and the first residents moved in on 16 May 1929. On 2 May 1930 the council decided to build a further eight houses and the process started again. By September 1932 one of the original tenants was in trouble with the council for not maintaining the garden in accordance with the tenancy agreement, and was told to put it in order or she would be served with a notice to quit. In 1946 another of the original tenants applied to the council for planning permission to add a cycle and a tool shed to the premises.[10] A drawing and ground plan of Amphtill's council housing can be seen in **colour plate 5**.

The 1935 Housing Act required local authorities to make an 'overcrowding survey' of houses in their area and report on 'houses unfit for human habitation'. The survey was co-ordinated by the Medical Officer of Health whose brief was to inspect all dwelling houses in his area that were occupied by the working class. In Cambridge it was agreed that the criteria by which these houses should be recognised was a rateable value of £13 or under. This amounted to some 12,000 houses in the borough, and included 2,000 council houses.[11]

Where the Overcrowding Survey has survived these will be found on cards in the county record office. Each card gives details of the house and its occupants. The information includes the address of the house, the name and number, ages and marital status of occupants, the name and address of the owner, number and size of rooms. This amounts to a census of working-class housing which makes it a valuable tool for the local historian. The long-term results of the survey and the records of the action that the authority took have usually survived and can be used as a surrogate if the cards no longer exist. These are the Registers of Unfit Houses drawn up as a result of the survey. The drawback is that although the survey covered all working-class housing the register does not, but using the 1921 and 1931 census returns the local historian should be able to work out what percentage of housing was placed on the register and draw some conclusions from this.

Registers of Unfit Housing give the address of the house, the name of the owner, whether this is a lessee or mortgagee, the name of the occupier and the number of residents. It should state whether the owner had agreed to improve the house or whether the council was taking action, and if the latter a date for the closure of the house and a note on where the occupants were being removed to should be given. Once more there is indirect evidence in these registers on the size of households, and direct evidence on landlords and the degree to which absentee landlords used houses to generate income.

Despite the state of some of the houses both owners and occupiers often objected to the demolition of their incomes and homes. When this happened a public inquiry was held, accounts of which appeared in the local press. In Cambridge such an inquiry was held in December 1936 at the Guildhall over the clearance of Cambridge Place, a narrow cul-de-sac of two-storey terrace houses which were home to 122 people. The Medical Officer of Health reported that none had inside WC's or a proper place to store food. All were damp and dilapidated. The inquiry revealed, however, that the houses belonged to a disabled ex-serviceman who depended on their rents for his income. Many of the tenants were old and could not afford to pay higher than the 2s 6d weekly rent, and did not want to move the two miles from the town centre where the council proposed to re-house them. They argued that they would not be able to afford the bus fare into the centre. Both owners and occupiers argued that the houses were sound, and although the street had a bad reputation (it often appeared in the local newspaper as the address of someone involved in criminal activity), it was now improved.

Another function of the local authority was to approve plans. In local authority records the local historian should find a plan register which gives the parish where the building is

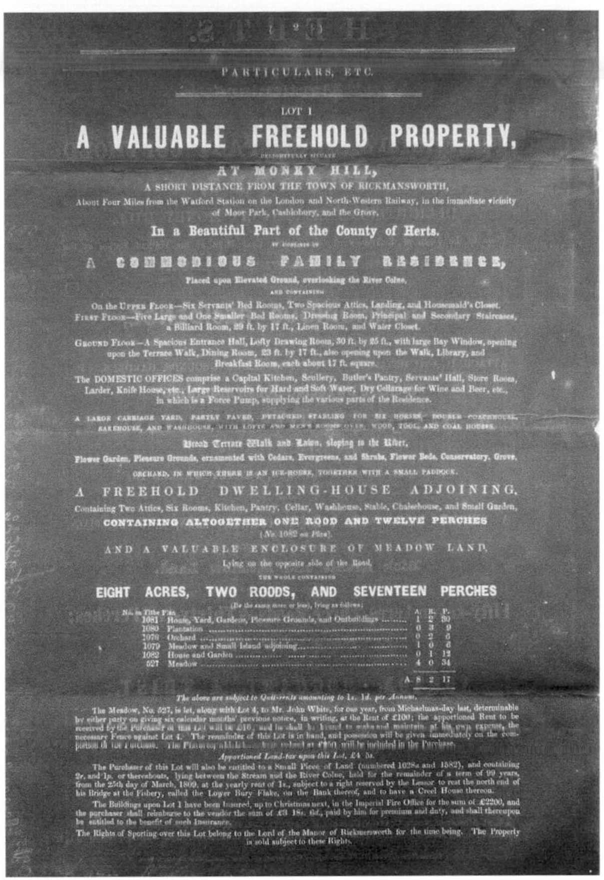
PARTICULARS, ETC.

LOT 1

A VALUABLE FREEHOLD PROPERTY,

DELIGHTFULLY SITUATE

AT MONKY HILL,

A SHORT DISTANCE FROM THE TOWN OF RICKMANSWORTH,

About Four Miles from the Watford Station on the London and North-Western Railway, in the immediate vicinity of Moor Park, Cashiobury, and the Grove,

In a Beautiful Part of the County of Herts.

IT CONSISTS OF

A COMMODIOUS FAMILY RESIDENCE,

Placed upon Elevated Ground, overlooking the River Colne,

AND CONTAINING

On the Upper Floor—Six Servants' Bed Rooms, Two Spacious Attics, Landing, and Housemaid's Closet.
First Floor—Five Large and One Smaller Bed Rooms, Dressing Room, Principal and Secondary Staircases, a Billiard Room, 29 ft. by 17 ft., Linen Room, and Water Closet.

Ground Floor—A Spacious Entrance Hall, Lofty Drawing Room, 30 ft. by 25 ft., with large Bay Window, opening upon the Terrace Walk, Dining Room, 23 ft. by 17 ft., also opening upon the Walk, Library, and Breakfast Room, each about 17 ft. square.

The DOMESTIC OFFICES comprise a Capital Kitchen, Scullery, Butler's Pantry, Servants' Hall, Store Room, Larder, Knife House, etc., Large Reservoirs for Hard and Soft Water, Dry Cellarage for Wine and Beer, etc., in which is a Force Pump, supplying the various parts of the Residence.

A LARGE CARRIAGE YARD, PARTLY PAVED, DETACHED STABLING FOR SIX HORSES, DOUBLE COACHHOUSE, BAKEHOUSE, AND WASHHOUSE, WITH LOFTS AND MEN'S ROOMS OVER, WOOD, TOOL, AND COAL HOUSES.

Broad Terrace Walk and Lawn, sloping to the River,

Flower Garden, Pleasure Grounds, ornamented with Cedars, Evergreens, and Shrubs, Flower Beds, Conservatory, Grove,

ORCHARD, IN WHICH THERE IS AN ICE-HOUSE, TOGETHER WITH A SMALL PADDOCK.

A FREEHOLD DWELLING-HOUSE ADJOINING,

Containing Two Attics, Six Rooms, Kitchen, Pantry, Cellar, Washhouse, Stable, Chaisehouse, and Small Garden,

CONTAINING ALTOGETHER ONE ROOD AND TWELVE PERCHES

(No. 1082 on Plan).

AND A VALUABLE ENCLOSURE OF MEADOW LAND,

Lying on the opposite side of the Road,

THE WHOLE CONTAINING

EIGHT ACRES, TWO ROODS, AND SEVENTEEN PERCHES

(Be the same more or less), lying as follows:

No. on Tithe Plan		A.	R.	P.
1081	House, Yard, Gardens, Pleasure Grounds, and Outbuildings	1	2	30
1080	Plantation	0	3	9
1078	Orchard	0	2	6
1079	Meadow and Small Island adjoining	1	0	6
1082	House and Garden	0	1	12
527	Meadow	4	0	34
		A. 8	2	17

The above are subject to Quit-rents amounting to 1s. 1d. per Annum.

The Meadow, No. 527, is let, along with Lot 4, to Mr. John White, for one year, from Michaelmas-day last, determinable by either party on giving six calendar months' previous notice, in writing, at the Rent of £100; the apportioned Rent to be received by the Purchaser of this Lot will be £16, and he shall be bound to make and maintain, at his own expense, the necessary Fence against Lot 4. The remainder of this Lot is in hand, and possession will be given immediately on the completion of the Purchase. The [illegible] valued at £[illegible] will be included in the Purchase.

Apportioned Land-tax upon this Lot, £4 5s.

The Purchaser of this Lot will also be entitled to a Small Piece of Land (numbered 1028a and 1582), and containing 2r. and 1p. or thereabouts, lying between the Stream and the River Colne, held for the remainder of a term of 99 years, from the 25th day of March, 1809, at the yearly rent of 1s., subject to a right reserved by the Lessor to rest the north end of his Bridge at the Fishery, called the Lower Bury Flake, on the Bank thereof, and to have a Creel House thereon.

The Buildings upon Lot 1 have been Insured, up to Christmas next, in the Imperial Fire Office for the sum of £2200, and the purchaser shall reimburse to the vendor the sum of £3 18s. 6d., paid by him for premium and duty, and shall thereupon be entitled to the benefit of such Insurance.

The Rights of Sporting over this Lot belong to the Lord of the Manor of Rickmersworth for the time being. The Property is sold subject to these Rights.

17 *Sale particulars, Rickmansworth, Herts.*

to take place, a description of it, registry number and the box number of the plan. The latter piece of information will enable the local historian to request the actual plan of the building. Plan registers include new houses and alterations to those already in existence. Also in local authority records are registers of property sales which date from 1900 onwards. These describe the situation of the property and what is being sold, the name of the proprietor and any persons who have interests in it, the date of the sale and remarks such as whether the property was sold by private treaty.

Connected with the sale of properties are sale particulars (see, for example, figure **17**), which can be found in county record offices, local studies libraries, and for up-to-date particulars look in estate agent offices and the property pages of the local newspaper. These usually include a description and picture of the property, sometimes interior as well as exterior, measurements, services, fittings, a map on how to get there, tenure of the property, price, rateable value or council tax band. Landed estate sale particulars will give details of all the properties on the estate which will include the extent of meadow, arable and pasture on each farm.

The documents created by the Finance Act of 1910, which placed a duty on land value, are an important source for local historians working on property. The records for this are found both in the PRO and in county record offices. This chapter is concerned with those records in the local record offices.

The act asked for local valuations of all property, which earned it the nickname the 'New Domesday'. The valuation books which form the initial stages of the inquiry should be found under the parish in the county record office. The information given in the valuation books includes:

Assessment and poor rate numbers
Christian names and surnames of owners
Christian names and surnames of occupiers
Description of the property: house
land
land and building
Street name and precise position of the property
Extent in acres or fractions of acres
Gross annual value
Rateable value
Extent as determined by the valuer
Original gross value
Reductions for buildings, timber, fruit trees
Original full site value
Fee farm rent, perpetual annuities value
Burden charges
Whether copyhold
Whether crossed by a right of way
Rights of common
Easements
Restrictions under covenant
Original total value
Deductions for works: Capital expenditure
Apportionments of land
Redemption of land tax
Release of restrictive covenants
Cost of cleansing site
Original assessable site value
Value of land for agricultural purposes when different from assessable site value

The valuation was followed by a form sent to the owners of land — form 4. Question six on this form has direct relevance to the local historian working on housing: 'description of land and particulars of any buildings and structures thereon, and the purposes for which the property is used'. Question eight asked about tenancy agreements, and nine whether the property was owner-occupied and what annual rent might be expected from it. Question 16 referred to details of the last sale within the previous 20 years and the amount of purchase money. The survival rate of form 4 is not as good as that of valuation books, and those that have survived are in a number of different places, but the county

18 Steeple Bumstead, Essex, 1960s (Haverhill Local History Collection)

record office should be able to locate the whereabouts of these. Working maps should also be found in the county record office, and form 37, which is a provisional valuation.

The information from form 4 and the valuation books was collated into field books which are in the PRO class IR 58. Item six of the field book is the gross and rateable value of the buildings, items 13–15 are on tenancy and rents, item 28 is a description of the buildings and 29 a sketch map of the building. Other information includes a description of materials used in the houses which enables the historian of vernacular buildings to identify local building materials and styles which may have disappeared by the late twentieth century.

The 1910 'New Domesday' is an invaluable source for the local historian. The problems and possibilities in using these have been fully explored by Brian Short in *Land and Society in Edwardian Britain*. The local historian can use these records for many different research projects that include a comparison of freehold and leasehold property. The extent of owner-occupation and land holding patterns in a parish, rateable values and the number of rooms in a house, can be used as a surrogate measurement for social structure, rents as a surrogate for the economic structure of a parish. Figure **18** shows the changing economic structure of a rural parish.

One of the difficulties the local historian should be aware of is the problem of scale, as another definition of the parish is introduced; that of the income tax parish as opposed to the civil or ecclesiastical parish. When parcels of land crossed the boundaries of these, the valuation staff invented yet another form of parish — the heridament parish.

19 Farmhouse in Nutfield, Surrey, 1930s

Case Study 1: Nutfield

Nutfield is a village in Surrey which straddles the greensand ridge either side of an ancient highway which is now the A25. The parish, which is long and narrow, stretches down onto the Wealden clay in the south. By the nineteenth century Nutfield was an industrial village with a Fullers Earth Works on the greensand ridge: however, the coming of the railway in 1842 shifted the emphasis to the south of the parish, and settlement started to develop around the railway.

The development of the south of the parish was largely the result of an initiative by Henry Edwards, who purchased the Kings Mill Estate and used parts of it to build villa housing for wealthy businessmen who could commute to the city from the nearby station, and also made land available for workmen's cottages on Trindles Road. The workmen's cottages were terraces of brick and tile houses. The 1910 valuation shows that many of these were owned by members of a local family, the Howicks, who had many interests and were part of a wide kinship network. Abraham Howick senior, who might be described as the patriarch of the family, owned 45 Trindles Road and the coal wharf by the station. His eldest son Abraham jr. owned stables at the end of Trindles Road and lived in another house in the road owned by his father. Another son Job, an engine driver, owned three houses adjoining the stables. Further up the road, other sons Victor and Oliver, and a daughter were owner-occupiers. These houses had a gross value of £11, a rateable value of £9 and a full site value of £205. The houses consisted of 2 living rooms and a kitchen downstairs with an outside WC, and 3 bedrooms upstairs. Outside was a small front garden and a back garden looking out across fields.

The valuation not only gives the local historian information about the housing stock and

20 *Farmhouse in Nutfield, Surrey, 1960s*

values of land in the Edwardian period, but indirect evidence on the proximity of kin and role of local families in home ownership (**19, 20**).[12]

Case Study 2: Gamlingay in 1910

The 1910 valuation books show that the houses in Gamlingay were owned mainly by absentee landlords or wealthy squires. Richard Astell, an absentee landlord, owned 72 heridaments including three farms and their land, and 44 cottages on the Heath, each accompanied by an acre or a fraction of an acre of land. Another substantial landowner was Colonel Duncombe who owned 41, or 17% of all heridaments. In Gamlingay there were only five, or 0.7 percent owner-occupiers in 677 heridaments. Other absentee landlords included Clare and Downing Colleges, Cambridge, and Merton College, Oxford. The latter had at one time been the major landowner in the village. Merton College leased the 115-acre Gamlingay wood to Colonel Duncombe as well as land and plantations in Old Woodbury, the Heath and Waresley Road.

A number of cottages in the village were owned by families living in Potton across the border in Bedfordshire. Table 17 illustrates this trend in Mill Street.

Table 17 Absentee Landlords, Mill Street Gamlingay, 1910

Owner	**Occupier**	**Description of Property**	**RV**
George Avery of Potton	A. Peters	Cottage	£3 8s
George Avery of Potton	G. Heath	Cottage	£3 8s
George Bartle of Potton	F. Jakes	House and shop	£8 10s

Sarah Bartle of Potton	S. Frances & S. Arnold	Cottage	£3 8s
Anne Bartle of Potton	G. Carter & A. Wade	Cottage	£3 8s
Sarah Bartle of Potton	G. Bruce & Mercy Stratton	Cottage	£3 8s

Many cottages in Gamlingay were in multiple occupation or were divided into two, which indicates a shortage of accommodation in the village. The overall impression from the valuation is a village of smallholdings, where cottages still had land attached to them, which may reflect the open field system of strip farming of the medieval period. There were also some substantial farms and a Mansion at Woodbury Hall. The housing in Gamlingay reflected a microcosm of the social structure of Edwardian England.

The valuation book also shows that Gamlingay was a close-knit community with families living in close proximity, for example in Richard Astell's cottages on the Heath were five households each of the Peck and the Darlow families.[13]

In 1971 a working group on housing needs issued a report on what was needed in the northern region. In 1975 another problem was recognised and investigated — that of second home ownership in the south west. A survey was made in 1977 of vacant property, and in 1979-80 a national survey on housing was taken. An inquiry into Local Housing Stock was held in 1985, and in 1986 postal questionnaires were sent out to ascertain the number of houses in multiple occupation. In 1988 there was a housing queues survey and in 1994 a housing attitudes survey.

As well as official records, and records produced when property changed hands, the local historian should also consider other avenues of research into housing. Housing associations are one area that has been under-researched, building societies are another, and charities that help the homeless will show the other side of the coin. Housing associations and building society records are probably still in private company archives, but both of these organisations have to be registered, so may be traced through the records of the registrar for building societies and the charity commission.

Neither should the local historian forget the houses themselves. A comparative study of Edwardian terraced houses needs to be made before these disappear, while little has been done to log types, sizes, and prices of new houses in the late twentieth century.

Finally it has to be admitted that for many in the late twentieth century, housing conditions have improved with more space and better amenities, but acquiring these was a hard-fought struggle, and they were eventually achieved through the co-operation of national and local government, and private endeavour.

4 Education

At the beginning of the twentieth century some form of elementary education was in place for the majority of children under ten years of age. The immediate concern was to provide education for children over that age, and as the century progressed, to revise and reform the education system. The state was heavily involved in this process and, as in the case of housing local and national sources, are meshed together. On a local level there are records pertaining to individual schools, whilst pupils' work and memories recorded on paper and audio tape show that schooldays were not always the happiest days of an individual's life.

The 1902 Education Act had a direct effect locally as it abolished the voluntary school boards and replaced these by local authorities, which were elected bodies. Responsibility for state education became a partnership between the local authority and the government, and many of the sources on education reflect this partnership. The local historian working on education will probably need to visit the PRO to look at state records, and will also have to bear in mind that education records that name individuals, attendance registers for example, are subject to closure orders from 30 to 100 years.

Information on education in the summary returns of the census of 1921 appears on table 15. The information given in this table covers counties, county boroughs, municipal boroughs, and rural and urban district councils, but does not go as far as parish level. The information is divided into age groups and sex, and then into the numbers in full or part-time education.

Table 17 Percentage of population in full time education in Derby and Exeter, 1921

	Derby: total population 142,403		**Exeter: total population 59,582**	
Age	**M**	**FM**	**F**	
0-4	0.3	0.28	0.3	0.33
5-9	4	4	4	4
10-14	4	4	4	4
14-19	0.1	0.2	0.5	0.5
20-24	0.01	0.06	0.25	0.14

Other information on education in the summary reports of the census can be found in the tables on occupation which give the figures for teaching as an occupation. In 1901 this was found on table 32 and from 1911–31 in table 15. The information was again divided into male and female, and for female teachers into married and unmarried. These tables illustrate the importance of unmarried women to the teaching profession. In 1901 in Suffolk, 67 percent of all teachers were unmarried women. By 1931 this had risen to 77 percent of all teachers. Many local education authorities operated a marriage bar which meant that women teachers had to leave the profession on marriage. The result was schools where the staff were predominantly young women with little experience, or mature unmarried women who had dedicated their lives to teaching.

The involvement of the state in education has resulted in a large amount of material being deposited in the PRO, class ED. Of importance to the local historian is ED 2, the parish files, which date from the nineteenth century. These contain reports and recommendations of the inspectors of schools, returns made by the local authority about the school, notices about the provision of classrooms, and plans for enlargements. The class is arranged alphabetically by county and within each county by parish. ED 2/248 is the parish file for Nutfield in Surrey. Nutfield School was a church school, situated on the greensand ridge on the highway which ran along its spine. By the early twentieth century this meant a two-mile walk up a steep hill for many of the children, as the centre of the village had shifted to the south. The parish files include a note on the population of the district, the number of children, and the amount of school accommodation which ought to be provided; in this case places for 210 children were needed. However, only 137 children were in the school, and the inspector thought that the deficiency should be made up by a new school built in the south of the village.

A shortfall of school places in the early twentieth century meant that many local authorities were seeking subsidies and permission to build new schools or enlarge existing ones. ED 7 contains the preliminary statements sent by the local education authorities to the Board of Education. These give details of the tenure of the school, the date it was built and the extent of existing buildings and accommodation. Details are also included on staffing, income and expenditure. ED 7/58 is the preliminary statement sent in by Middleton in Lancashire. It gives information on the authority's annual income for education and how this was obtained, whether it was from a local education rate, charitable subscriptions, the school pence paid by the parents or the authority's general fund. This is set beside expenditure on salaries, books, stationery, fuel, lighting and debts. The authority also had to furnish information on whether boys and girls were educated separately, whether the master and mistress were man and wife and whether the authority was asking for money to fund apprentice pupil teachers. It was also asked to supply the average number of children in each school. This latter piece of information is a way of obtaining numbers of schoolchildren in a school at a given time, even though it may not be possible to have access to their names.

Middleton Infant School was funded from school pence which gave it an income of £68 14s 9d, plus a grant from the general fund. It had two infant mistresses who were paid £30 4s a year and two assistants who received £10 8s and £2 12s respectively. £4 was spent on fuel and light and £3 on repairs. The school had 157 children on its books and wished to have permission to appoint a pupil teacher. The council also wanted to open a council school in Durnford Street (**21**) to be funded from the general fund. This was opened on 2 May 1910 and took pupils from the Central, Ward Street and New Jerusalem Schools. Maps and plans of the schools were appended and the school described in detail. The names and birth dates of the teachers were also added, and their length of service recorded. Further information on school funding can be found in ED 10, which includes letters from

21 *Durnford Street School, Middleton, Lancashire, c. 1925. (Reproduced by permission of Rochdale Libraries, Local Studies Collegion, Middleton)*

local authorities and returns of the local educational rates.

Attendance at school was a matter that caused both national and local government disquiet. ED 18 is the school attendance file, but because it often mentions individuals it has a 50-year closure on it. ED 18/400 is the attendance file for Bath. Sections 4-6 of the 1921 Education Act gave local education authorities the option of extending the age of compulsory education for children at public elementary schools at the authority's discretion. In 1929 Bath introduced a by-law which made education compulsory up to the age of 15. In October 1929 the Bath Education Officer wrote to the Secretary of the Board of Education that extending the age of compulsory education would raise the school roll in the city from 1785 to 1927. This would cause particular pressure in the West Twerton area, but no real difficulty was anticipated. A copy of the by-law was enclosed with the letter, and an exclusion clause, which allowed a child of 14 years who had suitable employment to leave school, was marked. The secretary of state thought that this clause was inconsistent with the terms of the Education Act and wrote to the Education Office. Eventually a compromise was reached and the clause was altered to between 14 and 15.

ED 18/641 shows Bath's education policy on exemptions in practice. In 1936 there were 660 applications for exemptions of which only two were refused. The majority of boys leaving school before the age of 15 became errand boys or messengers, whilst the girls went into domestic service. Towards the end of the 1930s a change can be discerned as boys given extensions were going into engineering and girls into the book binding industry of which Bath was a centre. Most exemptions were applied for immediately after the child's 14th birthday, and before an extension was granted the child had to have a medical inspection, a satisfactory school report card, and provide information on the nature of employment. A list was appended to the file of employments which were not considered suitable. These included working in the kitchen of a hotel, working in a billiard room or any place of information. The child was not allowed to do heavy lifting, and was to be paid a fair wage for the district, was not to work more than 36 hours a week and was to have a half day holiday and six hours a week off for further education. ED 18 also includes information on the attendance at public elementary schools. In the 1940s the information included the attendance by children normally resident in an area and the number of evacuees.

HMI reports are found in ED 51 primary, and ED 53 secondary. Staffing information is in ED 60. ED 60 is arranged first by county and then by local authority. ED 60/5/193B(i) is the staffing file for Jarrow. It includes correspondence and copies of letters sent to the authority and staffing figures for full-time teachers in public elementary schools, in this case from 1927–1936. Form 59E included in the file has information on class sizes and HMI recommendations on these is on Form E.N.116.

Table 18 Average Size of Classes in Jarrow 1926

Size	**No. of classes**
Not over 20	8
Over 20 not over 30	35
Over 40 not over 50	65
Over 50 not over 60	53

This indicates very large classes, on which the HMI recommended action. Question B on form E.N.116 was on overcrowding policy. The answer given by the HMI stated that Jarrow's policy was that no class should contain more than 50 children, and that boys in Standards IV-VII should be taught only by men.

A year later there was a significant improvement in class sizes with 87 classes containing over 30 but not 40 children, and only 35 with over 50 children in them. Increases in staff meant that class sizes continued to fall. Given the interest in class sizes in the late twentieth century these figures make an interesting comparison, and show that local authorities took what the HMI recommended to heart and made great efforts to improve the quality of education.

The re-organisation of education after the 1944 act produced new classes of records, especially with reference to secondary education. ED 196 are HMI reports on secondary schools. ED 196/5 is the 1947 report on Linton Village College. It gives a description of the college which was opened in 1937 as being housed in light and airy buildings surrounded by playing fields. However, the same room was used as hall, gymnasium and dining room, and there was not place in the classrooms to display charts.

One of the aims of a village college was to provide educational and social activities for adults, and to achieve this purpose an adult wing with a large common room and a canteen serving refreshments in the evening was added. Further education figures for the college show a steady rise in evening attendance from 254 in 1937 to 453 in 1947, but the report suggests that transport was a problem in the evening. Most adult students were housewives, but there were a significant number of farm workers. The most popular subjects were 'women's health' and 'current affairs' and the least popular were French and music.

Further information on adult education can be found in ED 73. ED 73/3 is the file on the University of Cambridge Department of Extra-Mural Studies, now the Board of Continuing Education. Included in the reports is a mention that at Isleham and Over, village history groups had been formed as a result of classes held by the university with the aim of collecting material for publication. The Isleham group had already compiled an account of the village over the last 100 years. Other information on adult education is in ED 68 which covers adult residential colleges from 1911–35. ED 71 deals with state scholarship awards for students going into higher education 1910–44. In 1911 there were 200 state scholarships which rose to 360 in 1936. At the other end of the age scale, ED 69 contains nursery school files.

Local records on education can be divided into local authority committees, which decide policy, and education departments, which put the policy into practice. Before the 1944 Education Act primary schools came under the borough, rural or urban district council, but secondary schools were part of the county or county borough's responsibility. After the 1944 act the county had responsibility for state education at its three stages of primary, secondary and further. The county's powers extended to providing milk and meals, board and lodging if necessary and ensuring good hygiene by banning pupils infested with vermin, or in 'a foul condition'. Transport had to be provided where essential, and the county also had to fund teacher training.

County council records should include the printed minutes of the Education Committee and its various sub-committees, for example on agricultural education or special education. Departmental records will include minutes and papers for divisional executives, which were in place from 1902–74, registers of teachers' salaries,and, available up to 1947, letters and reports from school managers. Building programme files, publications on and about the school and files of illustrations may also be available in county or other local authority records.

Records of church schools will be found in the county record or diocesan record office. In many counties church schools have formed their own association and these records should be lodged with the county record office.

Turning to the schools themselves, details of actual buildings will be with the appropriate architects department, where plans and illustrations should be found. After the school boards were abolished in 1902 many counties took a survey and made a plan of the schools they took over, and these will be contained in the records of the county architect. The other main classes of records from schools will include notices of school holidays, admission registers, managers and trustees records. All of these have a 50-year closure order on them.

The most important document to come from a school will be its log book which is a day-to-day record of events in the school kept by the head teacher. These were started in the nineteenth century and many continued into the 1950s and '60s, although it has to be noted that there is a 50-year closure order on these.

Where log books are available they give a detailed account, not only of life in the school, but also in the area in which it was situated, but the degree of detail given in the log book depended on the diligence, interest, and time available to the head teacher, so that some log books contain more information than others. Using log books the local historian will be able to compare the fluctuating attendance at the school and identify newcomers to the school and its area. Dates and results of inspections, tests, and examinations are given, as are the results of school football matches and sports days. Information on the teaching and other staff is given, news about school excursions, open evenings, fire drills and the state of the weather. It is impossible to generalise about the quality of the information because each book is an individual record, one can only recommend that the local historian seeks out examples to see what they contain.

As well as official records on education, the second half of the twentieth century has seen a growth in voluntary bodies associated with education, for example parent-teacher associations. Individual parent-teacher associations are part of county federations, and even if the records for individual schools are not available the federation records should have been deposited in the county record office. These records will include minutes of meetings and correspondence. Some counties also have 'school journey' associations which were founded in the 1950s. Deposited records of these include minutes, bulletins and accounts. These will help the local historian to reconstruct the extra-curricular activities of schools. Also deposited in county record offices are the minutes and correspondence of county societies for the extension of university teaching which helped to organise evening lectures for adults. Local branch material for the Campaign for the Advancement of State Education, which began in 1962, may also be found in the county record office, as should material from local branches of the Workers Education Association, the Co-operative Society's education branches, and the records of non-Conformist Sunday Schools.

It is only recently that attention has been paid to the role and status of the actual providers of education, the teachers. Log books give some clues as to this, but other indications can be found in trade union records. County branch minutes, reports and papers of the National Union of Teachers are in the appropriate county record office while the Modern Records centre of the University of Warwick has records of the Assistant Masters and Mistresses Association. The records of the Association of Science Masters and Women Science Teachers are in the Brotherton Library of the University of Leeds. These include some branch records, and minutes books for branches in London, Liverpool and the northern areas.

Returning to the receivers of education, the children, records on education for the youngest of these can be found in the papers of the Nursery Schools Association, which since 1973 has included the National Society for Children's Nursery Education and the British Association for Early Childhood. These are kept at the headquarters of the association. Other records that the local historian working on education will find helpful include those in the British and Foreign School Archive Centre, which include the archives of training colleges in Stockwell, Saffron Walden and Darlington. In these records are student magazines, prints, plans and photographs and examples of students' work and samples of dissertations (**22**). These add another dimension to the local history of education as they illustrate the academic and practical preparation the teacher received before graduating to face a class of 40 to 50 children.

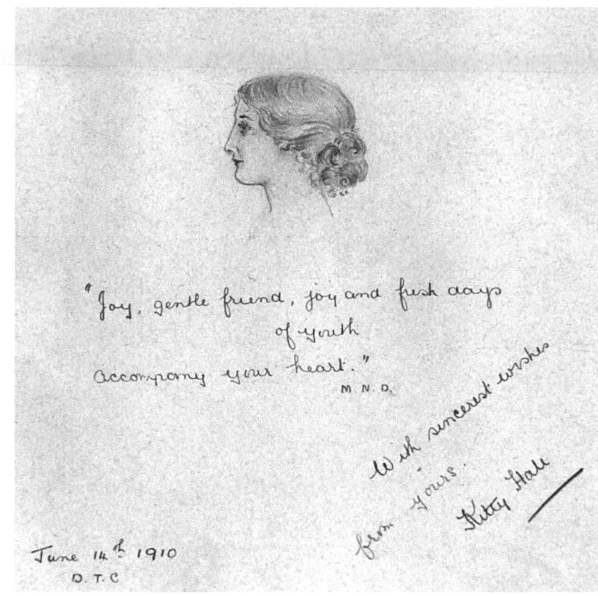

22 *Autograph book of pupil teacher, Bishop Lonsdale's College, Derby, 1910*

Case Study: Harston Church Board School in Cambridgeshire[1]

Harston is a village which straddles the A10 some five miles from Cambridge. In the early twentieth century it was an industrial village with several cement works in the vicinity, as well as coprolite digging and a mill. Now it is mainly a commuter village, although there are still some industrial plants in the area.

The school was opened in 1852. The school log book which records the day-to-day events starts in 1856 and is available for consultation in the county record office up to 1956. As well as providing education for children in the day the school also ran evening classes for adults. The first entry in the log book referring to evening classes is 1896.

As the environment in which the children were taught and the working conditions of the teachers could affect the whole educational process, plans are important in giving dimensions of rooms and facilities. They are also important as they enable the local historian to compare the past with the present, especially as many of these schools have now changed their use, and are private houses or small workshops. As well as the county architect's plans, written inside the school log book are the dimensions of the schoolrooms.

The school had three rooms:

Schoolroom 37ft 6in x 20ft
Class room 18ft x 15ft
Infants room 20ft by 18ft

In 1900 the school had five teachers. Mr Beaumont the head teacher was a certified teacher, three women teachers were articled teachers, and one, Beatrice Ashby was a candidate for pupil-teacher training. The average attendance at the school was 120. This gives a ratio of 30 children per teacher, which compares favourably with the class sizes given for Jarrow earlier in this section. Using a combination of local and national records the local historian could map class sizes for the early twentieth century and look for regional trends which could lead to a study of how class sizes affected children in later life.

School re-opened on 24 September 1900 after the summer holiday, or as the headmaster called it the 'harvest holiday'. This term is a good indication that it was not a time of leisure for the children and those that were old enough would have been working on local farms helping to get the harvest in. Probably some children returned to work after school had started, as by 10 October 1900 the headmaster noted that attendance notices had been sent out to parents.

In the winter of 1900–1 the school was severely hit by illness amongst staff and pupils. Such was the severity of this that it was noted by the HMI when he visited the school on 4 August. Beatrice Ashby passed the candidates examination in May 1900 and we can follow her career through the log book. The report on her shows that she was a satisfactory teacher of history, geography and reading, but weak in English language and music. On 18 February 1901 the headmaster received a complaint about her for striking children, and recorded in the log book that he had spoken to her very firmly. During her period as a pupil teacher the school manager's minute book reveals that she earned £2 10s a month and attended the Cambridge Pupil Teacher's Centre for which she received a season ticket for the railways paid for by the school managers. She completed her apprenticeship on 30 June 1904 and was appointed assistant teacher at Shillington near Hitchin. Apart from the one complaint about her, she had a successful career as a teacher and in June 1927 spent two weeks back at the school helping and advising the infant teacher.

We can appreciate that Beatrice Ashby may have had difficulties with the children she was teaching as not so long before she had been one of them, and she had several younger relatives in the school. One, Frank, was given corporal punishment in June 1902 for striking, kicking, swearing and calling the teacher names. However another, Annie, was awarded a needlework prize in October 1902, and Ashby was a common surname in the log book throughout the early 1900s.

The log book indirectly records the movement of population into and out of the village as children were entered or withdrawn from the roll. The roll started to fall in 1904 and stood at only 88 in 1908 and 61 in 1927. It did not start to rise again until after the Second World War and by 1956 stood at 172. This increase meant that the school was severely overcrowded, and the infants class was held in the village hall.

The log book records staff changes, special events and in great jubilation, honours accorded to the school when a child was awarded a county scholarship to attend a county secondary school. This was flagged up in the log book by HONOUR and the child's name, girls as well as boys. The log book also notes problems with the buildings, holidays and school closures and events like Empire Day with a description of the celebrations.

There is evidence in the Harston log book that the classrooms were not adequately heated, for example on 26 January 1917 it records 'ink frozen in the ink wells'. The head master kept a record of the temperature in the infants' room over the winter, and also records the running battle with the county council to get the stoves in the classrooms repaired, as often these filled the rooms with smoke and the children had to be evacuated. The HMI's reports, and bouts of sickness are entered. These not only included epidemics such as measles or mumps, but outbreaks of ringworm. Evidence of local customs appear

23 Empire Day 1920, St Johns School, Redhill, Surrey

in the log book. In the early 1900s many boys were absent from school on Plough Monday which was the second Monday in January, and the girls were absent on St Valentine's Day. These absences disappear from the log book after 1905 and appear to have been replaced by Empire Day (**23**). Absence from school was condoned for the choir, church or chapel outings and when the district flower show was held at Harston.

National events impinged on the school. In the 1914–18 war one of the teachers who was a volunteer Red Cross worker was working all night in Cambridge tending wounded soldiers from the front, and teaching all day in the school. The headmaster applied for exemption from military service but was refused and while he was in the forces a series of substitute head teachers kept the log book. Harston school became a junior mixed infants in 1947, and in 1959 seniors were transferred to Melbourne Village College.

One of the functions of the local authority was to provide ancillary educational facilities such as libraries. In the early years of the century the public library provided worthy but often dull books on a closed access system. The reader chose the book and the library assistant then fetched it. There was no browsing along the shelves, and the librarian could censure what was given to the reader. Gradually readers were issued with their own tickets and allowed to chose up to three books, of which one or two had to be non-fiction, thus reinforcing the didactic nature of the library.

The public library service started thanks to the generosity of a Scottish migrant to Canada, Andrew Carnegie, who gave small local authorities money with which to set up a library service. The 1919 Public Libraries Act made the Board of Education responsible for these and enabled county councils and county boroughs to borrow money in order to create library services.

Information about the library service can usually be found in the library sub-committee of the County Council Education Committee. These minutes will contain statistics about books issued, additions to the book stock, books provided for evening classes, and special collections. Information on staffing reveals that most branch libraries were staffed by volunteers with perhaps a paid member of staff visiting once a week. In the late 1940s branch libraries began to acquire salaried members of staff, but the system was to be revised again in the 1960s when many county councils started to introduce mobile libraries and static branch libraries disappeared. In May 1964 the first mobile library set out across Cambridgeshire. On the first day 718 readers enrolled, so it might be accounted a success, except that now readers could only use the library once a week or once a fortnight, and then only for a limited period, whilst the cramped nature of mobile libraries made browsing along the shelves impossible.[2]

Some library sub-committees include details of books that were purchased or withdrawn from the library. The borough of Cambridge had a books sub-committee which dealt with this. The minutes of this reveal some interesting facts about what the authority thought the reading public should be given. At the end of the 1920s the book sub-committee started to withdraw or put on restricted access books which revealed the full horror of the First World War. Books such as Robert Graves' *Goodbye to All That*, E. Guedella's *Slings and Arrows,* and R. Aldington's *Death of a Hero* were withdrawn from open access and only the librarian could decide who could borrow them. The books sub-committee also read any books which might be considered immoral and decided whether the library should buy these. On the positive side the minutes of the books sub-committee do reveal the purchase of reference and rare books which now form the nucleus of the Cambridge Central Library's special collections.[3]

Other information on reading habits can be found in the chief librarian's annual report, and in surveys of reading habits taken by, amongst others, the Mass Observation Survey. The local historian should not forget that there were lending libraries which were not part of the local authority's provision. Boots the chemist ran a subscription lending library in its bigger branches for many years, while smaller shopkeepers had shelves of books that could be borrowed for a few pence. Literary, philosophical, archaeological and antiquarian society libraries cater for intellectual tastes. Often detailed catalogues of these exist, with records showing what was borrowed and by whom. The collections of books themselves may be now an important part of the public or local studies library. Villages also had their own reading rooms.

Library buildings were the responsibility of the county or borough architect, and plans and information will be found in the architects' files. Not all of these were purpose built. In the 1950s and 60s the public library at Redhill in Surrey shared its premises in the Colman Institute with a billiard hall, which refused admittance to women.

The public library service plays an important part in the education and leisure activities of the local community in the twentieth century, and although activities have become diversified, the role of the book and the written word has not been diminished. Without the collections held in local studies libraries the historian would find the task of research on any period difficult, thus the public library should receive attention from those working on the local community.

5 Law and order

Throughout the twentieth century law and order has been a matter for public concern. Each generation has declared an increase in crime, and what it has perceived as a decline in public and private morals. Those charged with maintaining law and order at a local level have been alternatively respected and reviled, and the legal system has been held up to mockery. But is this necessarily the case across the country? The local historian is well placed to examine general statements on law and order through detailed local study, which may reveal trends that contradict the national pattern. Clive Emsley points out in his book *The English Police*[1] that too often historians have used the Metropolitan Police as a model for the structure of the police force, whereas the records reveal that it is the exception rather than the rule.

Law and order can be divided into the legislature that makes the law, those who enforce the law, the courts which try those who may have broken the law, and the places of custody where those found guilty end up. As with most aspects of life in twentieth-century England these functions are a mixture of public funding, private enterprise and voluntary involvement. Each of these produces records, but because of the sensitive nature of the material, much of it is closed to access, especially where it concerns individuals who are still alive.

Until the 1947 Police Act the local police force was very much an autonomous unit controlled by the local authority. This gave each police force individual characteristics. It also means that up to 1947 police force records are likely to be found in local collections, either deposited in the county record office or retained by the force and kept in Constabulary Headquarters.

The Metropolitan Police are controlled directly by the Home Secretary, therefore the majority of their records are in the PRO class MEPO, but there is also a Metropolitan Police Archive.

Local police forces were formed by the 1839 County Police Act. This converted the system of voluntary village constables into a professional force with a recognisable uniform, controlled by a chief constable who reported to the Justices of the Peace. But it was not until the 1856 County and Borough Police Act made it obligatory for the local authority of either the county or the borough to create a police force that the whole country was covered. The result of the 1856 act was a great number of very small police forces spread across the county with no uniformity. The 1888 Local Government Act rationalised this by abolishing police forces in boroughs with populations of less than 10,000, thus reducing the number of police forces from 231 to 183.[2] The 1947 act merged the smaller forces still in existence, reducing the number of forces by 45.

24-5 *The rural policeman as family man at leisure and on duty, Kensworth, Bedfordshire, c.1905. The policeman is Fred Stanbridge who died in 1908 at the age of 29 as the result of an accident. His wife Ada lived on until 1937. They were married in Clifton Baptist Church. The children are Grace, Bernie, and Bessie who was born in 1905. (Bedfordshire and Luton Archives and Records Service)*

Before the 1947 act was drafted an inquiry into local conditions of service was held. The report that followed this recognised the individual nature and lack of uniformity in local police forces. It asked each Chief Officer of Police to furnish details about local rules and discipline codes, and it provides a good guide to police attitudes at that time. The report quotes the 1925 regulations for married police; 'a constable may not marry without the previous consent of the Chief Officer of Police'. Some forces had detailed conditions on this, often not allowing constables to marry while on probation or requiring that 'the constable must produce references as to the character of his intended wife'. The report recommended that these restrictions should be abolished. There have been some oral accounts from police wives that voice how in rural areas a wife would become an unofficial constable when her husband was absent. The experiences of police wives and their families would make a fruitful area for the local historian to study.[3] A policeman as family man and on duty can be seen in figs **24–5.**

Police records can be divided into those about the control and administration of the force, reports on it in action and the day-to-day records generated by maintaining law and order in the local community. The first of these are to be found in county or borough council records. The county council usually had a Joint Standing Committee on Police. The minutes for this body are available in the appropriate county record office. These include discussions of police matters such as personnel and funding, and this body received the reports of the chief constable. In the borough council, responsibility for the police was usually in the hands of the Watch Committee. Minutes of Watch Committees show that they discussed a wide range of topics related with the police which will give the local historian information about the everyday running of the force.

In 1904 the minutes of the Watch Committee of the Borough of Cambridge included approval of gratuities given to police for meritorious conduct and special service. These included awards to PC 18 Wright, Sergeant Gates, PC 12 Unwin and PC 14 Savidge for keeping the fire at the Rose Hotel under control. The constables received rewards of 7s 6d and the sergeant 10s 6d. This is a case where record linkage can round out the events as the fire was reported in the local newspaper. PC Wright was commended again on 24 January 1904 for stopping a runaway horse.

One of the most important events in 1904 for the Cambridge Borough Constabulary was a royal visit. On 8 February 1904 the Watch Committee authorised the purchase of six swords for mounted police and £20 for a new uniform and ceremonial sword for the chief constable to be worn during the visit. Much time was taken up discussing the route the visit should take from the station and the practical necessity of supplying refreshments to constables posted along the route. It was all over by 7 March 1904 when the Watch Committee reported with relief that the arrangements had been satisfactory and all the constables were to receive an extra day's pay. Again this event can be linked with accounts in local papers, and the local historian has the opportunity to use an event like this to see what went on behind the scenes.

The Watch Committee minutes reveal that this was the body which received complaints about the police, and claims for damage to property during street disturbances that the police had failed to control. Throughout the first decade of the twentieth century claims for damages followed 5 November celebrations that had got out of hand.

The phrase 'taximeter cab' first appears in the Cambridge Watch Committee minutes in May 1908. The development of the motorised cab and local regulations controlling it is still a largely unexplored area and the Watch Committee minutes make a good starting point for such a study. Watch Committees everywhere became increasingly involved in

26 *Special Constables, Eaton Bray, Bedfordshire, 1940s. As can be seen, the Special's uniform at this time consisted of a hat and an armband. (Bedfordshire and Luton Archives and Records Service)*

traffic regulations as the twentieth century progressed. In March 1914 the AA and RAC sent a joint circular to all Watch Committees asking them to sponsor by-laws regulating slow-moving traffic, making the use of mirrors compulsory on heavy covered vehicles and making it compulsory for every vehicle to have a rear light.

In 1914 Cambridge Borough Police purchased their first police dogs, two Airedales. The use of dogs in the police, and the training of dog handlers in different forces would add to the understanding of police methods, and is a project that a local historian could undertake using Watch Committee minutes, chief constables' annual reports and police records.

Special constables were appointed during the First and Second World Wars. These were often retired policemen, but the Cambridge Specials included college servants and labourers. Instructions on how to behave were sent to them by the chief constable in August 1915. They were told that 'constables are placed in authority to protect and not oppress the public', and should not interfere without good cause. Their actions should be firm and decided. 'A timely and kindly caution, of which note should be made, often meets the case in a slight offence, but a second offence should be reported to the Magistrate.' Instructions included not loitering or gossiping on the beat, keeping out of public houses and checking the security of banks and jeweller's shops. They were instructed to leave a private mark on such doors so that they could see if they had been tampered with, and to observe unusual noises such as the breaking of glass or barking dogs.

Although stating the obvious these instructions are an example of many similar pamphlets to be found in local studies collections and give the historian some idea of the concerns of the chief constable. Note the emphasis on the protection of property in this pamphlet, and the desire not to give the public offence by heavy-handed policing. A group of special constables can be seen in figure **26**.

The Watch Committee received the annual reports of the chief constable. These were in printed form and are in the public domain, probably to be found in the local studies library or county record office. The chief constables' reports include returns of criminal and other statistics, and reports on the activities of the Fire Service and the Motor Ambulance Service for which the police were responsible.

Table 19 Comparison of the size of police forces in four counties 1901-21

	1901	**1921**		
County	**N. in Force**	**N. in Force**	**% Increase**	**% Pop. Increase**
Herts	423	600	4	3
Lancs.	6183	8160	4	0.5
Leics.	375	591	6	13
Lincs.	476	481	0.1	2

Chief constables' reports also give the cost of policing a borough or county and statistical information about rateable value, acreage of area covered by the force and the length of the streets that the bobby on the beat pounds every day. Other information includes information on alien registration certificates, bicycles lost and restored to their owners, numbers of stray dogs, and information on the licensing of peddlers, chimney sweeps, hotels, inns, beerhouses, theatres and cinemas.

Crime statistics are also in the reports, but are sometimes issued as a separate supplement. Offences are divided into indictable and non-indictable. Using these figures over time will enable the local historian to look at the question of increased crime over the twentieth century, and to identify trends in the types of crime. There is a notable increase in violent crimes as the twentieth century progresses, which confirms many of the worst fears expressed in the later years of the century. The clear-up rate can also be estimated from the figures and compared over time.

One type of crime that increased over the twentieth century was that connected with road traffic. In the early years of the century this was likely to be related to the use of bicycles, but later motoring offences predominate. Over half of non-indictable offences committed in the borough of Cambridge were for motor offences. The chief constable's report started to include a special section on motoring offences and accidents from the 1920s onwards. In the case of fatal accidents a description of the event is included and by the 1960s photographs of the scene.

Increased motor usage changed the structure of the police. The 1930 Road Traffic Act introduced motor patrols in many forces, and the details of the vehicles purchased for the police are given in the chief constables' reports, as are details of traffic controls. The reports of the chief constable for the borough of Cambridge reveal that the borough had six sets of automatic traffic signals by 1934. In that year the chief constable noted that 'Persons — mostly cyclists — are still passing the signals when the *amber* light is showing'.

Indictable offences connected with motoring included theft of motor vehicles, which increased steadily through the 1930s, as did non-indictable offences such as exceeding the speed limit or causing an obstruction. In the 1950s police forces started to try to educate the public in road safety with campaigns across the country, which included the police visiting schools to make cycle inspections. The growth of modern policing can be traced through the annual reports made by the police. A growing awareness of the importance of good public relations and a workable complaints procedure is evident in most reports.

There is also a great deal of material available on the day-to-day running of the police force. This covers administration, personnel in the force, police funding and responsibilities, and perhaps most interesting for the local historian, records of the everyday activities of the police station and in some cases individual policemen or women.

Records on the police themselves include personnel registers, pay books, lists of pensions, complaints and discipline books, dismissal books, regulations and instructions. Records on the police in action will be based on each station and may include charge books, summons books, previous convictions records, notes on identification parades, station logs, photographs of criminals, cell books, beat books and the station daily log book.

Examples from Bedfordshire of the information in some of these sources are given below. Although Bedfordshire is the county chosen for this, the records were standardised and the same information should be available across the country.

In order to detect a crime it had to be reported to the police in the first instance. The record of crime contains the details of the report made to the police. Each station kept a record of crimes reported and each should contain:

No. of entry
Date and hour of report of information to the police
Date at which reported to the Inspector
Name and occupation of person reporting
Alleged time and particulars of the crime or offence reported
Estimated value
Proceedings for recovery (if property) and apprehension of offender
Amount recovered
Amount not recovered
Page in report book
Proceedings against the offender
Whether convicted or discharged

This example comes from the record of crime of the Bedfordshire Constabulary (Leighton Buzzard and Woburn Division)

> 25 November 1930 at 12.30 report made by the School Authorities at Carlton of the theft of a bicycle and cape belonging to S.L., bricklayer. Reported to the Inspector on the same day.
>
> S.L. who was working at the Carlton Training School left his bicycle against the

1 *Poster advertising the benefits of living in Letchworth Garden City*
Photograph by courtesy of the First Garden City Heritage Museum, Letchworth

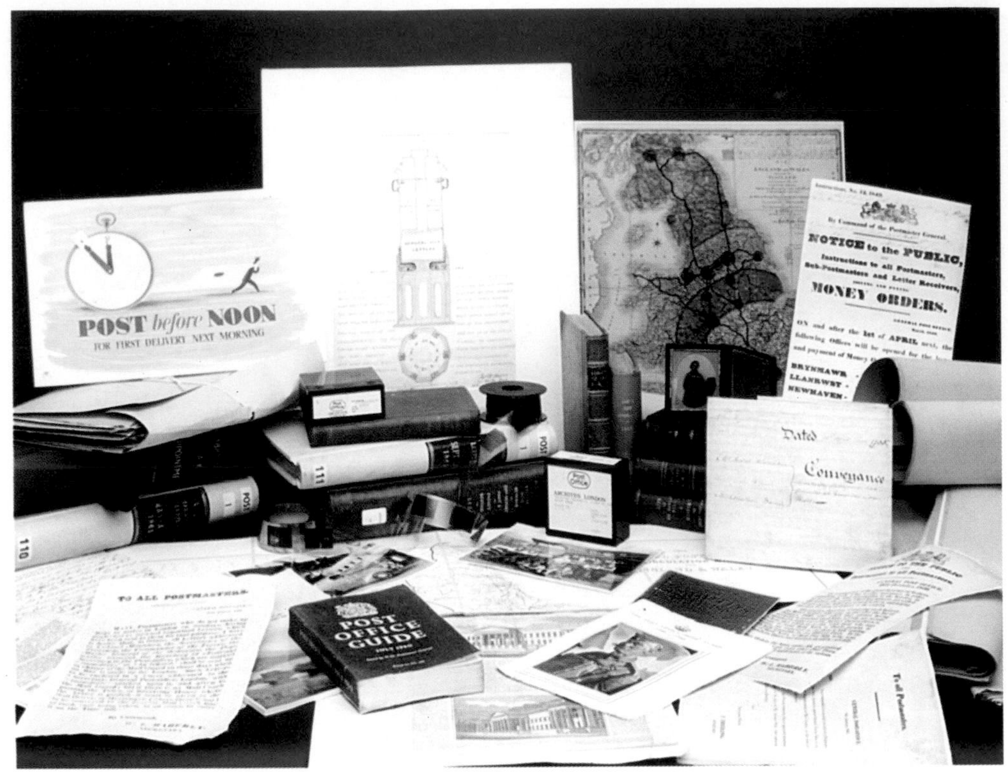

2 *A selection of sources at The Post Office Archive*
Copyright The Post Office. Reproduced by permission of The Post Office

One Lord, One Faith, One Baptism

He that Believeth and is Baptized shall be Saved.

Roland Frederick Ernest Jordan

was Baptised

at R.M.A. Church Eastney

by the Chaplain

on November 21st 1909

SPONSORS

Frederick Robert Jordan

Earnest Peter Jordan.

Signed H.S. Wansbrough Chaplain R.N.

THE PRESENTATION

By one Spirit are we all Baptized into one Body.

Baptizing them in the Name of the Father and of the Son and of the Holy Ghost.

No 127. S.P.C.K.

JOHNSON, RIDDLE & Co LTD LONDON, S.E.

3 *Baptismal certificate*

4 *New Eastwick, Yorkshire: houses built by the Rowntrees for their employees at the beginning of the twentieth century*
Courtesy Dawn Tivey

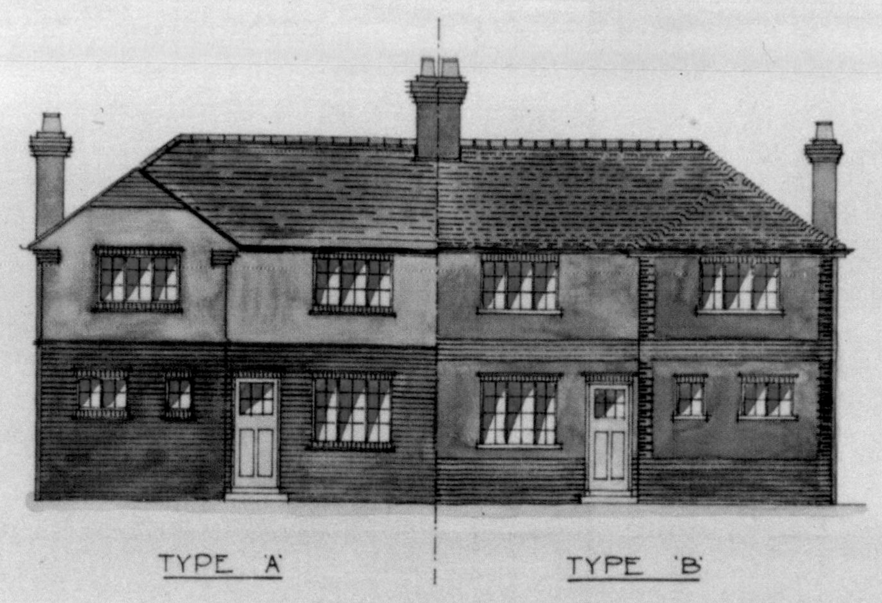

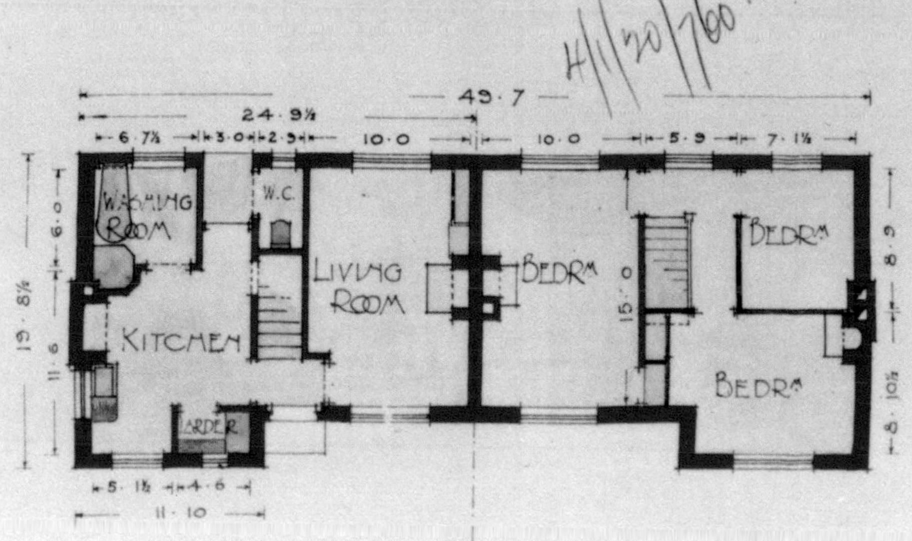

5 *Plan of council houses, Ampthill, Bedfordshire*
Courtesy Bedford and Luton Archives and Records Service

6 *Early twentieth-century village street*

7 *Slum clearance: overcrowding in the back streets of Chesterfield, Derbyshire, 1960s*

8 *Bathing beauties at Scarborough, c.1920*

9 *Seaside scene in Eastbourne, early twentieth century*

10 *Canal at Bath, 1996*

11 High Peak Railway, 1965

12 Remains of the High Peak Railway, 1994

13 *The twentieth century invades the countryside: Staffordshire moorlands, 1980s*

14 *Power station*

15 *Grave of Charles Day, d.1916*

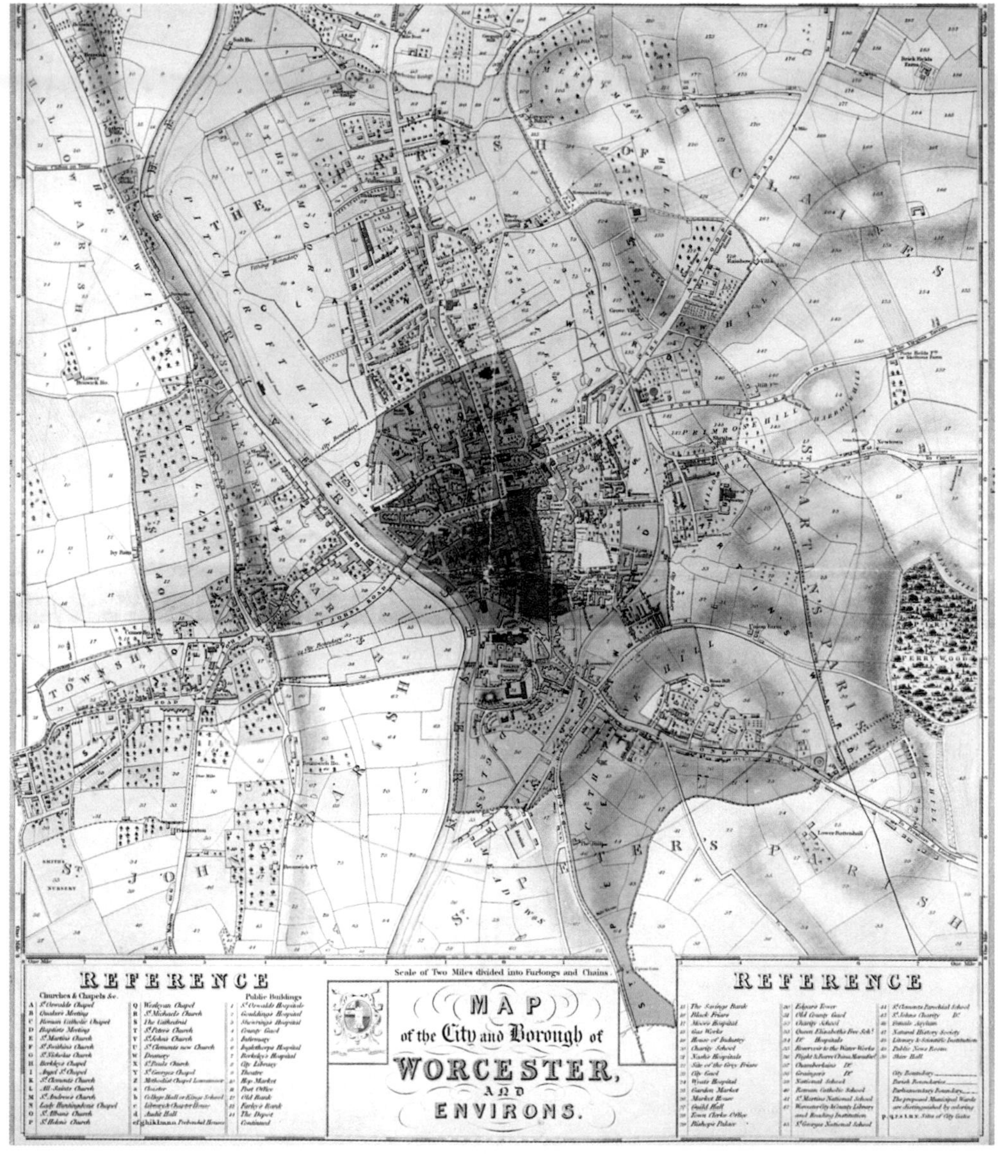

16 *Map of the city and borough of Worcester and environs*
Copyright The Post Office. Reproduced by permission of The Post Office

17 *Laxton open fields, 1993*

18 *Mixed farming in Derbyshire*

19 *Norbury parish church, Derbyshire. Once the heart of the village, the parish church lost its importance in village life as the twentieth century progressed, but it is still usually the oldest building in the village*

20 *A modern records centre: the Library, University of Warwick*
Courtesy the University of Warwick

21 *The Search Room, The Post Office Archives*
Copyright The Post Office. Reproduced by permission of The Post Office

> main gate of the school. It was there at 11.00 but gone by 1.40. The bicycle was a Royal Enfield with an old farm cape strapped to the carrier. Value £7 10s.
>
> On the same day A.S. aged 14½ absconded from the school (this was an approved school). He was seen riding the bicycle at Turvey Smith apprehended and returned to the school. All the property was recovered.[4]

Using the record of crime book the local historian can build up an intimate picture of crime and how it affected individuals in the local community or, using a more statistical methodology, to examine seasonality of crime across a year, or changes in the pattern of crime over a number of years.

Another version of the record of crime was the general report book kept by each station. This was made by the constable investigating the crime or incident. It gives the date of the report, the particulars taken on the reported incident, the places where constables inquired about the crime and remarks on this.

Here is an example, in 1925, from the General Report Book for Sandy in Bedfordshire, 1925:[5]

> PC 35 reports that on Saturday 12 September he received information from A.C. a market gardener of High Road, Beeston, Sandy that between 5p.m. and 7a.m. 1cwt bag of King Edward potatoes value of £1 8s had been stolen from his field at Tempsford north of Blunham beside the Great North Road.
>
> PC 35 proceeded to the field and was shown the position in which the potatoes had been left overnight when the men left work. He made inquires at Tempsford, Sandy and district without result. Enquiries were continued but no information could be obtained.

PC 35 would also have kept a beat book. The beat book contained the number of the beat, the boundaries of the beat and its description, points where the constable was to stop, time of relief and times of refreshment periods.

Once apprehended, an offender was charged and a register of charges was kept by each station. Each charge was given a number and contained the following information

> Name of person charged
> Age
> When charged
> By whom
> Address and occupation of person charged
> Nature of charge
> When the accused came before a magistrate
> At which office fine paid.
> How the charge disposed of
> Sentence
> Property found on prisoner
> How this property was disposed

These examples come from the 1903 Bedfordshire Constabulary Charge Book, register of charges (Dunstable)[6]:

> **No. 999**
> H.S. aged 40, charged by Inspector Pickering of Dunstable on 15 August 1903 for unlawfully moving a pig into the County of Bedfordshire without a licence. (No address or occupation given). Fined 7s 6d. Paid.
> **No. 1000**
> G.S. aged 37, labourer of Dunstable Road charged on 21 August by Patrick Doone of Bedford for unlawfully treating a horse to the point of exhaustion. Fined 10s and costs of 7s 11d. Paid.
> **No. 1002**
> M.C. aged 21 of West Bridgeford charged on 22 August by Ada B of Dunstable as being the father of a bastard child. Order made to pay 3s a week for 13 years and to pay 30s in cash immediately.
> **No. 1003 and 1004**
> W.M. aged 32 peddler of Dunstable and his wife aged 31 charged on 23 August by Inspector Boydell of unlawfully neglecting 2 children. Committed for trial at the assizes.

Police records contain information on members of the force. It is possible not only to trace their careers, but their backgrounds, physical appearance, date they married and when they left the force. The record of service book for each county constabulary gives:

> Name, age, height, complexion, hair, particular marks, where born (in or near which town), county, trade or calling, single or married (marriage date added if after joining the force), number of children, residence, what public service, regiment, length of service, amount of pension, with whom last employed, when discharged, if ever in police service before, date of appointment and number, division and dates, beat, date of removal from the force, remarks.

W.H. was born on 14 June 1908. He was 6ft 1in and had a fresh complexion, brown hair and no particular marks. He was born in North Shields and was living there when he applied to join the Bedfordshire Constabulary in 1929. He had been a soldier before applying to join the police force having served with the Coldstream Guards from 1926–9. He was discharged from the army in October 1929. He was single when he applied to join the force but married on 3 November 1934. He was appointed to the Bedfordshire Constabulary as PC39 on 16 January 1930 and served first in Luton. In 1933 he transferred to Biggleswade but returned to Luton where he was stationed at Barton in 1935. In 1937 he moved to the Riseley division. He took and passed the sergeants' examination on 12 May 1939. His salary on joining the force was £3 10s and had risen to £4 6s 9d when he was made up to sergeant.[7]

This biography of one member of the police service can be multiplied many times. Each biography can tell the local historian about the background of those joining the service,

27 *The Old George Inn, Bedford. (Bedfordshire and Luton Archives and Records Service)*

their age and whether they were prepared to move to join the police. Their movements while in the force can be plotted.

Parallel to the record of service book is the conduct book which deals with those who infringed police regulations. This contains the name, age and height at joining the police, the date and nature of the offence and by whom reported. Details of the punishment are given and remarks. But as well as dealing with offenders the conduct book also deals with those who were 'noticed' or 'rewarded', recording the date of the event, the way in which the police man or woman distinguished him or herself, by whom this was noticed and the amount of the reward.

Further information on life in the police may be found in quarter sessions records which may include details of police pay, nominal rolls of those in the service, sick register, annual review of the strength of the force and the police pensioners lists.

Also contained in police records are a number of social documents which give the local historian information about the community in which the police worked. These are found in registers of licences issued, which include licenses to hotels, public houses, inns and beerhouses, as well as licences to chimney sweeps and peddlers. The register of fully licensed houses and beer houses enables the local historian to trace those houses which have disappeared, to see who held the licences and what accommodation was available. The register contains:

The sign of the house
Situation of the house and its rateable value
The name of the owner

The name of the original licensee
The date the licence was transferred and to whom
Date forfeited
Disqualification of premises
Number of public and private rooms in the house
If for the use of the public whether bedrooms, sitting rooms
Amount of stable accommodation
Cautions for misconduct
Nature of complaint and by whom cautioned
Date of caution
Record of criminal proceedings
Date when licence first issued
Date when house closed.

Using this register the history of the licensed house can be traced.

The Old George in Bedford's High Street was an old established inn (**27**). Its rateable value was £42 in 1896, which had risen to £64 in 1928. It was owned by Mary W. but the licence holder was Walter Firmin, butcher. The licence was transferred to Henry Whitbread in 1896 and to Edward Moore in 1904. Henry Whitbread took it over again from 1907–19 when it passed to Abraham Weethurst who was licensee from 1919–28 when Henry Thunis became the licensee for only a brief period before the house was closed in 1928.

The Old George was a house of ill repute and this may have been one reason for its closure. During the First World War it was banned to airforce personnel, and the licensee was fined more than once for serving them. In April 1920 the licensee was cautioned for allowing obscene language in the bar. In July 1922 he was summonsed for allowing betting on the premises, and in July 1927 for encouraging rowdiness and allowing persons under the influence to remain on the premises, which resulted in a fine of £2 plus 7s 6d costs.

More sedate was The Midland Hotel first licensed in 1869. In 1896 the hotel was owned by Newland and Marsh of Lurke Street Bedford with James Hatcher as its licensee. The licence was transferred to Thomas Gatteley in 1908 and to C.W. Pamplin in 1936. The hotel had 11 rooms of which there were two public bedrooms, three public sitting rooms, and stabling for seven horses. Like the Old George it fell foul of the Defence of the Realm Act in 1916 and was fined for selling drink after hours to members of the military.[8]

Grocers and refreshment houses also needed licences issued by the police. The information contained in the register of grocers and refreshment houses includes the address of the premises, the name of the owner, the name of the proprietor, the date of the original licence and the date and to whom transferred, cautions for misconduct and proceedings taken. This information enables the local historian to trace shops and their owners, where these were situated and what they sold. For example in 1901 a licence to sell sweets and wines in a shop at 14 St Paul's Square Bedford was granted to Samuel Finch. The shop was owned by W. Wood of the High Street and the licence taken over by Joseph Deppen in 1906. By 1908 the licence had lapsed and the shop sold only sweets.[9]

28 J. Hockle, chimney sweep, Biggleswade, Bedfordshire. (Bedfordshire and Luton Archives and Records Service)

Registers of pedlars' licences give the name, age and address of the licensee, who granted the licence, date of the grant, date of expiry and the fee paid. This was usually 5s a year. The chimney sweeps register not only gives the name and dwelling place of the licence holder but also the names of those employed, and whether journeymen or apprentices. A Bedfordshire chimney sweep can be seen in figure **28**. One feature of these registers that the local historian must bear in mind is that licences were renewable annually so that there is much repetition.[10]

In the first half of the twentieth century designated policemen were also auxiliary firemen and the chief constable had to report on the activities of the fire brigade giving details of the calls attended and the machinery the fire brigade owned (**29-30**). In many towns this was very antiquated and included hand carts carrying pumps. Rural areas were particularly badly served unless there was a volunteer parish fire brigade. In August 1941 local fire brigades became part of the National Fire Service, and after 1945 local authorities divided the police and the fire services. The police maintained law and order on the ground. Those they apprehended and charged underwent the process of the law through a system of courts. The Lord Chancellor is the head of the judiciary, and records produced by the Lord Chancellor's office are in the PRO. The Home Secretary administers magistrate courts and has overall responsibility for police and prisons. Class HO are the Home Office records in the PRO. The records of the Attorney-General, who acts for the crown in the public court, the Crown Prosecution Service, and the Director of Public Prosecutions have 100-year closure on them. The central criminal courts, or the Supreme Court of Justice created in 1873, include the High Court, the Court of Appeal and the Central Criminal Court. The latter is known familiarly as the 'Old Bailey'. Records from

29 Horsedrawn fire engine, Haverhill, Suffolk, c.1900. (Haverhill Local History Collection)

30 Suffolk Fire Service, 1950. (Haverhill Local History Collection)

the latter are in the PRO class CRIM. These include CRIM 2 — the calendar of prisoners which has indexes of cases sent up from local magistrates courts. CRIM 4 contains jury lists, and CRIM 6 court books, which contain summary details of trials and offences. All of these have a 75-year closure order on them.

Local court records will be found in the appropriate county record office. Until 1971 the highest local court was the Assize Court held by a peripatetic judge travelling on a circuit from court to court. In 1971 a major overhaul of the court system abolished the assize in favour of the Crown Court, and the quarter and petty sessions became magistrates courts. Class LCO at the PRO is a list of magistrates. These records have a 75-year closure on them.

Other local courts include civil courts such as the small claims courts and the coroners court which inquires into sudden deaths. When using court records the local historian must preserve the anonymity of anyone involved whether accused, witness or police, and most local court material has a 30-year closure on it. If this rule is observed there is much valuable material available in the county record offices, which will not only help the local historian to reconstruct individual cases, but also to examine types of crime and relate these to social conditions. In working on this line of inquiry the local historian will be able to add to the wider sociological debate on the causes of crime and its relationship to poverty, unemployment and the environment.

Records connected with petty or quarter sessions will include the Clerk of the Peace's Letter Books. These reveal the behind-the-scenes business of the local courts. The letter book will contain a copy of the letter sent and the reply received. Subjects covered include the commitment of prisoners, drafts of trial proceedings sent to prison governors receiving the prisoners, notices of fines imposed and received and notices to appear at court to receive sentence, notices of hearings, lists of evidence received and lists of charges.

Quarter sessions record books for the twentieth century will include lists of justices appointed for each session, a calendar of indictments for each session, sentences meted out if the defendant was found guilty and costs of the prosecutions. Also appended will be a list of summary convictions made when the defendant did not appear to plead, or pleaded guilty. If a session was held when no indictments were heard this was entered in the record book as a 'maiden session'.

This example of the type of indictment heard at the quarter sessions come from the Cambridge Borough sessions held in October 1910:

> Crown v. Daisy X who broke a plate glass window in Kings Parade worth £9 and committed other damage worth £5 against the peace. Pleaded guilty. Detained under penal servitude in a borstal for two years.

Using the quarter sessions record books the local historian can compare lengths of sentences meted out both within the same session and over time, and look at the way in which different justices dealt with the same crime. The Cambridge Borough sessions appear to have given women and juveniles harsher sentences than men, even when the man had previous form. The case recorded after the unfortunate Daisy was of a man accused of deception and falsely detaining goods worth £10 by claiming that his son had no employment but could get work if he could hire a horse and cart for a day, and then detaining it. It transpired that he was already wanted on a similar count in Staffordshire, but he received six months imprisonment whereas Daisy's term was three times as long. In 1912 a woman was accused of the theft of a blouse worth 2s and also received a two-year sentence, and in 1936 a young women was found guilty of stealing a dress, petticoat and shoes from the Sisters of Mercy for which she received a three-year sentence.

Obtaining clothes by false deception was a common crime in the 1920s. The accused usually acquired mourning clothes by telling sympathetic but gullible shop assistants that the clothes were needed urgently for a bereaved but impoverished relative who had expectations of receiving a legacy from the deceased, when the clothes would be paid for in full. Having obtained the clothes these were then sold. One confidence trickster took in the largest stores in Cambridge, the Co-operative Society, Eaden Lilley and Robert Sayle and Co., with a 'story that his wife had a death in her family and needed a black dress which she would pay for out of a £50 legacy'. A false name and address were given, and in each case the defendant claimed to be a fish merchant. One cannot help but admire the irony in this, whether intended or not, as surely the sales assistant should have recognised this as a 'fishy' story.

A large number of cases in the first half of the twentieth century in Cambridge and in other courts dealt with the theft of bicycles. Breaking and entering was also high on the list. It was common for the accused to ask for other offences to be taken into account from other towns across the country, and tracing the location of criminal activities suggests that from the 1910s onwards the criminal class was extremely mobile.

In February 1932 the Cambridge Borough Court tried a man for the theft of a Hoover Suction Cleaner worth £20 19s, for which he received 12 months' imprisonment. Electrical equipment listed as stolen items appears more frequently from the mid-1930s onwards.

The quarter and petty sessions tried mainly petty crimes against property, but some crime against persons also appear in the record books. For example, actual bodily harm and assault against women, ill-treating children and indecent assaults on both men and women were tried by the justices. The more serious of these were referred to the assizes or to the crown court.

One of the functions of the clerk of the peace was to compile calendars of prisoners. There is a 30-year closure on these calendars, and care must be taken to preserve the anonymity of individuals mentioned in those which are released. Provided that this is observed these are interesting documents that give short life histories of the prisoners in a way which invites comparison with the settlement examinations taken under the Old Poor Law 200 years earlier.

Calendars of prisoners may be loose sheets or in bound volumes, each volume covering the session at which the prisoners were to appear. The information given includes the name, age and occupation of the prisoner, and if a juvenile the age of the parent. Previous convictions and sentences are listed in date order with the location where these occurred. This helps to trace personal mobility across the country. For example a prisoner at the Cambridge Borough sessions of 1935 had commenced a criminal career in north London.

31 Crowd outside Bedford Prison, 1905. (Bedfordshire and Luton Archives and Records Service)

From there he went to Manchester, Stratford (East London), Chelsea, Liverpool, Essex, Liverpool, and from there to Cambridge. The offence that the person is being tried for is described, the name of the Justices of the Peace who heard the case, and the sentence given.

A sample from the May 1948 calendar of prisoners for Cambridge shows that there were 14 prisoners of whom two were women. Their ages ranged between 17 and 62, but over half were aged between 17 and 21. Five of the prisoners were airmen from nearby bases, and those sentenced included a German POW who was to be deported at the end of his sentence. Eleven were accused of breaking and entering, two of stealing money and one of gross indecency with another male. Convictions for the latter were to increase. In the 1963 spring session seven of the 16 prisoners were charged with gross indecency with another male. The local history of the gay community in the twentieth century has yet to be written. Calendars of prisoners are a convenient starting point for such a study. The question that might be asked in this case was whether the police were taking the moral high ground while the justices were more broadminded? The sentences given were ambiguous and included conditional discharges, probation and in two cases the charges were dismissed. This would be an area where the court records would need to be read in conjunction with local newspaper reports and editorials. The other crimes being tried at this session included sexual intercourse with a minor, and motoring offences. There were no women in this group of prisoners and their age range was wider than those in 1948 with five over 40.

When a jury was needed, the Clerk of the Peace had to draw up a list of jurors. Again there is a 30-year closure on these, but as the jury lists include name, place of abode, age and occupation it is possible to look at the composition of juries for different sessions.

The final set of records to be discussed, which are found in the quarter session records are the quarter session bundles that are arranged by session. These contain a full record of the indicted, the charge and the evidence. The bundles also contain the list of the jury that heard the trial, newspaper notices announcing the dates of the sessions, a copy of the calendar of prisoner for each case, letters from prisoners in mitigation, a record of the examination of the prisoner by the police, a copy of the charge sheet with the police evidence, and lists of witnesses and their depositions. Also in the bundle will be the cost of the hearing and the sentencing order and a copy of the general order given to the police on their position at the sessions, the dress they were to wear and the time they were to be on parade. Each case produced at least ten separate documents, and these are an under-utilised source on local life.

If the sentence given at the end of the trial is custodial, the ultimate destination of the accused is prison. Throughout the twentieth century there has been a debate as to whether prison should be an instrument of punishment or of rehabilitation and training. These questions are especially relevant to the treatment of young offenders.

In 1900 an experiment began in Bedford Prison (**31**) which introduced a programme of moral and practical instruction for young offenders that it was hoped would make them fit for a more profitable and law-abiding life at the end of their sentences. These ideas were developed in an institution specialising in young offenders at borstal in Kent, and this place gave its name to the whole system. Young offenders were also sent to industrial and reform schools which became known as Approved Schools, under the 1933 Children and Young Persons Act. There were also institutions for re-training young offenders run by charitable organisations such as the Royal Philanthropic Society School, at Redhill in Surrey. The records of this institution are in the Surrey County Record Office, and county record offices hold a great deal of material on local reform or training schools.

Population size is a factor that must be borne in mind when looking at figures which suggest there is an observable rise in the number of prisoners in an area and by implication a rise in crime. Variations in local conditions were emphasised in the Criminal Registrar's report for 1903.[11]

> The county is a useful, and for some purposes an inevitable unit. But within the same county may be the most diverse conditions: a high rate of criminology and a low; a population very dense in some parts, sparse in others, and very different rates of marriages and births, mortality, and amount of school accommodation. Certain towns affect the returns for the whole county; outside them or their zone of influence returns may be very different.

This is a useful reminder for local historians working on a variety of topics.

6 Entertainment, sport and leisure

One of the characteristics of the twentieth century has been the growth of leisure time for the mass of the working population. By the beginning of the century the August Bank Holiday was a well-established feature and most workers had Saturday afternoon as a legitimate half-day. A paid holiday was not, however, a statutory requirement until the 1938 Paid Holidays Act. The increase in workers' leisure time and a rise in real wages has led to a commercialisation and centralisation of leisure activities with a change from locally funded activities to theatre, cinema chains covering the whole country, and a rise in national and professional sporting leagues. Other revolutionary changes in the world of leisure were to alter the fabric of everyday life. The growth, first of sound broadcasting and later television, turned leisure activities inwards on the home.

A leisure activity that has survived over many generations is convivial drinking in an inn, tavern or public house, despite the expense.

Table 20 Prices of Drinks Sold in Public Houses in 1907

1 dozen large bottles of Bass	3s 6d	per dozen
1 dozen small bottles of Bass	2s 6d	per dozen
Gin	3s	a bottle
Irish Whisky	2s 6d – 4s	a bottle
Scotch Whisky	2s 6d – 4s 6d	a bottle
Brandy	2s 6d – 5s 6d	a bottle
Rum	2s 6d – 4s-	a bottle
Claret	1s – 3s	a bottle
Port	1s – 3s 6d	a bottle
Ginger Beer	1s 3d	per dozen bottles.

Table 21 Beer Consumption per head in gallons[1]

1901	32.5
1939	19
1949	21.5
1959	16.6
1969	20.3

Duty on beer fluctuated widely throughout the twentieth century, but this did not deter drinkers.

Information on drinking habits can be found in the Mass Observation Archives File 3016, which is an outline report on drinking habits taken in July 1948 when 9,000

32 Bottling Department, Biggleswade Brewery 1930. (Bedfordshire and Luton Archives and Records Service)

people were interviewed. Some interesting facts emerged about local drinking habits that the local historian might find interesting to test on other areas. For example, in the heavy industries at Middlesborough bitter was drunk to replace sweat lost at work, but in the Midlands mild was the preferred drink. Women were more likely to drink Guinness partly because of a current advertising drive which associated Guinness with health.

Many brewery records have survived. Some are deposited with the county record office and others are kept by the brewery, which may, like Bass of Burton-on-Trent, have their own archive and museum. Brewery records enable the local historian to trace take-overs, the demise of small breweries and the encroachment of outside concerns and large combines on the local public house. A good example of this is the activities of Greene King Ltd of Biggleswade (**32**) which sought to enlarge its territory by buying up smaller concerns in Cambridgeshire and Essex, and through this gained access to customers not only in these counties but in Northamptonshire and Hertfordshire as well.

The records of Hudsons Brewery, one of the breweries which became part of Greene King, show the process in action. These records show that in the early years of the twentieth century Hudsons was equally predatory, and that it was in the first two decades of the century that many small breweries disappeared. One of these was the Worboys Brewery, which in 1909 had a mortgage of £4,500 on the Coach and Horses at Harston, The Sailor's Return at Meldreth, The Anchor in Melbourn High Street, and The Plough in Little Shelford, as well as The Cuckoo in Sandon, Hertfordshire, when it sold these houses 'with goodwill and interest' to Hudsons. Six years later Worboys went into

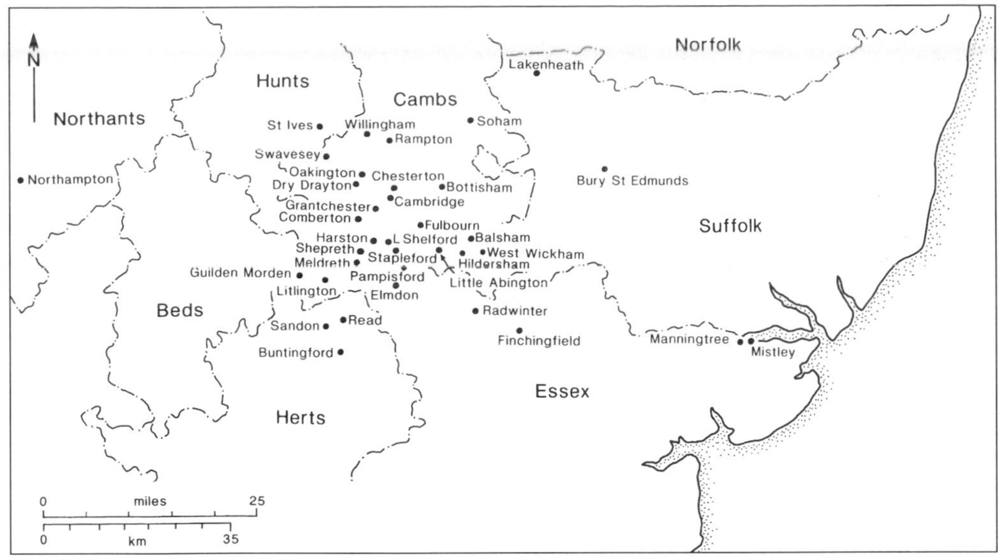

33 Location of Hudson's Brewery, public houses, Cambridge, in 1920. This map illustrates the delivery problems encountered by small breweries

receivership.[2] The extent of Hudson's activities is shown in figure **33**.

What happened to some of Hudson's houses is shown below:

> Anchor Beer and Wine House, Melbourne. Purchased from Worboys 1909, Sold to Barclay and Perkins of London 1921, re-sold to Wells and Winch of Biggleswade 1938.
>
> Skinners Arms, Manningtree, Essex. Sold 1921 to Barclay & Perkins, 1938 purchased by Wells and Winch, 1947 sold to Cobbolds of Ipswich.
>
> Spotted Cow Northampton, acquired by Hudsons in 1898, withdrawn and sold in 1905, repurchased in 1906 with money from the sale of the George and Dragon in Willingham, Cambridgeshire.
>
> Prince Albert and Isaac Newton, Castle Street, Cambridge acquired 1899, amalgamated as the Isaac Newton in 1929 and as such still exists.

The sale of Chesterford brewery and its eight public houses took place on 20 August 1913. The brewery which had brewed 2,900-3,000 barrels in 1912 consisted of a steam brewery, two maltings, a malt house, engine, boiler, cooperage and clerks office. This indicates that even a small brewery would have been a major local employer and that closing down such a concern would throw many local people out of work.

The public houses being sold included The Flower Pot at Duxford, Cambridgeshire, The Plough at Birdbrook in Essex, and The Five Bells in Saffron Walden. The sale details describe the house, the materials it was made of, number of rooms, outbuildings and the position of the privy. Chesterford Brewery was purchased by Hudsons and later came into the hands of Greene King. Brewery records are likely to include conveyance deeds, sale details and insurance papers as well as account books, minutes of board meetings, register of employees and other material relating to the running of a firm.

Perhaps one of the most essential sources for the study of public houses in the twentieth century is the public house itself. The sign of the house can tell the local historian something about the history of the area and the date of the public house, which might be confirmed by the date of the building.

Social drinking in public houses has remained a popular pastime but the numbers attending live theatre have fallen across the twentieth century. Many professional theatres have closed or changed their function.

Licence books give details of the premises occupied by theatres and cinemas while the minutes of county council theatre committees show who issued licences for public performances, to whom and for what. Often the request for a licence included a plan of the building and the committee had a right to inspect the premises. The minutes will mention any improvements that the committee deemed necessary.

The following are extracts from the minutes of the Cambridge County Council Theatres Committee:

> 15 March 1913. A licence was issued to enable Perse School to perform stage plays for the public.
> 29 May 1913. A licence was issued to the Conservative Hall, Soham to enable them to show cinematographic films. On the same day a licence was given to J.A. Chipperfield of Gamlingay to show performances in a moveable structure.
> 16 October 1913 A licence was given to the ADC theatre for the performance of stage plays. This theatre in which all performances are by amateurs still presents plays and operas to a devoted audience.

The same committee renewed the licence for the New Theatre in St Andrews Street, Cambridge and noted that there was to be no smoking in the theatre during the performance. If theatres were not commercial ventures they were probably part of a trust, and the records of the trusts may be deposited with the record office. These will include correspondence, accounts minutes and details about the premises. Commercial theatre management companies have also left records, and from these it is possible to trace circuits of plays travelling from theatre to theatre.

Theatre records in general have survived in fairly large numbers, and are often found in private homes as people are reluctant to throw away mementoes of evenings out. These items include photographs, programmes and posters. Reviews and advertisements can be found in the local newspaper. The local historian will be interested in the offerings of amateur dramatic and operatic groups. Many of these have deposited their records with the local studies library or county record office. These will include playbills, programmes, photographs, accounts, minutes, details of costumes and properties and the rules of the

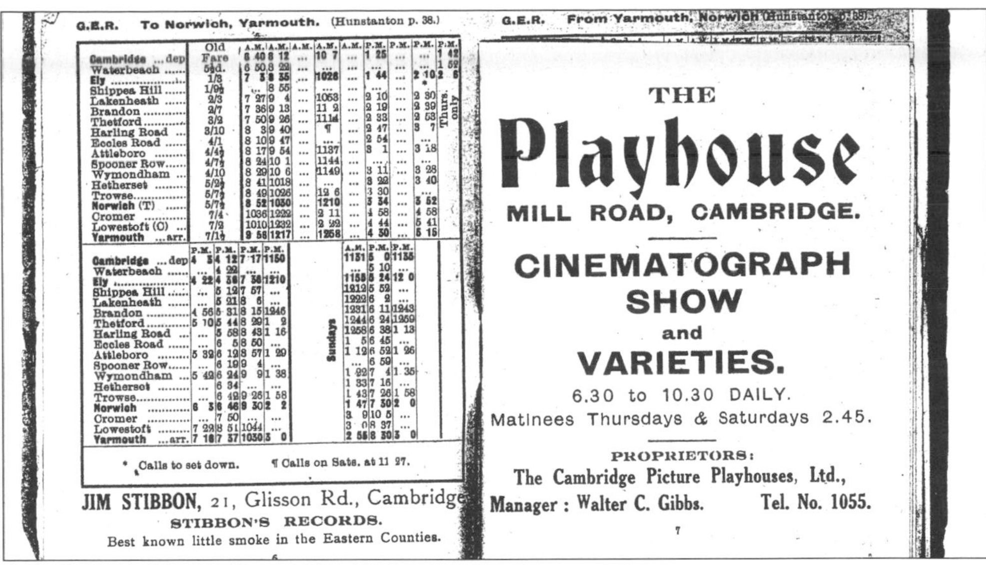

34 *Advertisement for The Playhouse, Cambridge, showing how the cinema and the theatre existed side by side*

club. Local festival programmes should not be ignored, and the local historian should note who sponsored the festival.

One reason for the decline of live theatre was the cinema, which quickly captivated audiences, although at first the two existed in the same venue (**34**). By 1914 there were 3,000 cinemas in Britain, licensed under the 1909 Cinematograph Act.

After the 1909 act the Cinematographic Licence was issued by the local justices at the petty sessions. Details recorded included:

Number of the licence and its duration
Name and address of the person to whom it was issued
Situation and description of the premises
Whether it was a permanent enclosure or a temporary building
Cubic space
Seating capacity
Number and dimension of exits
Dimension of any stairs
Nature of lighting
How the building was ventilated
Alterations to building
Particulars and date of lapse of licences
Special terms and restrictions.

It also included the terms by which the justices issued the licence. The Ely and Witchford Division justices stipulated that cinemas must be closed on Sundays and on days

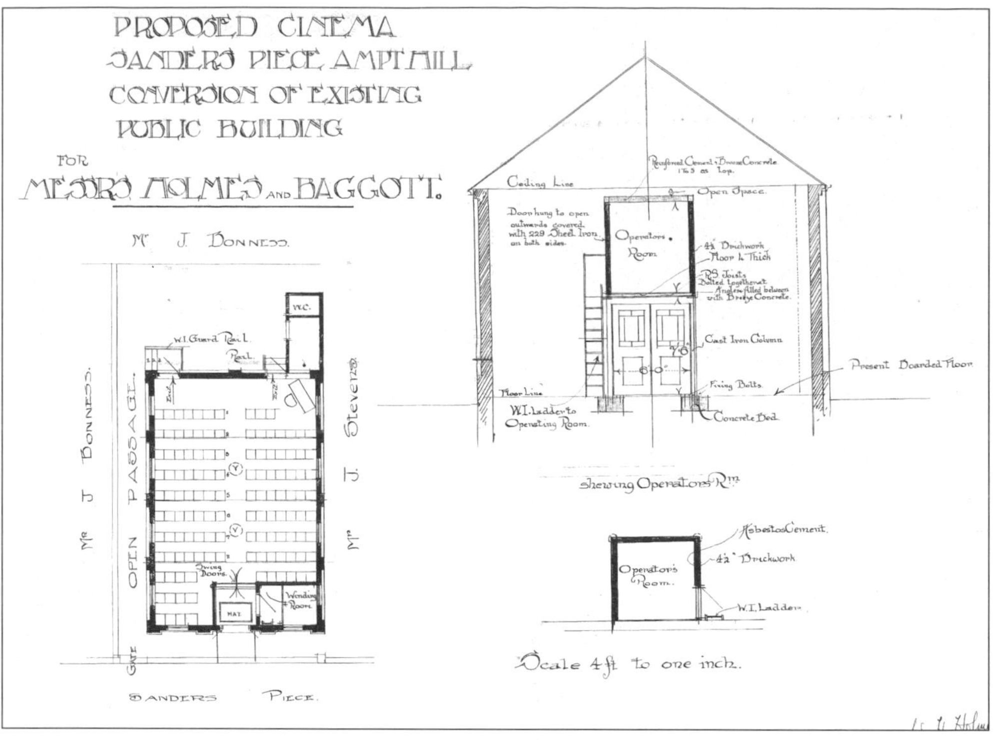

35 *Plan of a cinema, Ampthill, Bedfordshire. Note the reinforcement of the operator's room. (Bedfordshire and Luton Archives and Records Service)*

appointed for public thanksgiving. The audience had to be out of the cinema and the doors locked by 11 each night, no liquor was to be sold without a special licence, and police, whether in uniform or plain clothes, had the right to be admitted by the manager at all times during a public performance. The manager was at all times to maintain good order and decent behaviour in the building, and would be fined £20 for each contravention.

After a series of disastrous fires in cinemas across the world, additional clauses were added which forbade the use of combustible material in the auditorium, and eventually detailed instructions were issued on how the projection room with its highly inflammable film and equipment was to be isolated from the rest of the building.

Other clauses added concerned the types of film shown. No film could be shown which was likely to be injurious to morality, encourage or invite crime, lead to disorder or offend public feeling by offensive representations of living persons. If the Licensing Authority deemed that a film contravened these standards it could not be shown.

The Ely and Witchford Division licensing book shows that licences were not confined to the towns, but cinematographic performances were shown in villages and hamlets. The local historian can use the licensing book to trace the spread of the cinema across a region. The first licence issued by the Ely and Witchford justices was to Thomas Bolton of Fox Hill Ely for the showing of cinematographic films in the gymnasium hall, Victoria Street

36 Inside a prefab, 1947. Still from a film. (East Anglian Film Archive)

Ely. The licence was valid from 16 March to 31 December 1911. The building itself was 57ft x 34ft and 16ft high and could seat 250 persons. It had two outside doors, both opening inwards which were to be fastened back during the performance. There were no stairs and the building had a wood boarded floor, and shutters ventilated the projection box. The cinema was warm and comfortable. It gave a feeling of luxury and because alcohol was not allowed on the premises it was somewhere for the family to visit together, whilst the darkness gave a welcome privacy to the courting couple. Cinemas were to become more and more luxurious. The Odeon chain built elegant art deco cinemas across the country, while other cinemas imitated local stately homes, and the facilities were extended to include restaurants and tea-rooms. Plans for new cinemas had to be approved by the local council and can be found through the appropriate register of plans. The plan will give the name of the owner and the architect and include a seating plan (**35**).

Part of the programme included newsreels. In the early cinema these included local events such as the local agricultural show or opening of a hospital. These and other cinematographic records of local life have been collected by regional film archives and are valuable resources for the local historian. They show features which written records do not, such as clothes and body language, and they also show changing land and townscapes. The aims of the regional film archives are to 'search out and preserve moving images . . . and where possible to provide a service of access and presentation'.[3] Figure **36** is a still from the East Anglian Film Archive.

One effect of the commercial cinema which the local historian might be interested in pursuing is its role in the Americanisation of local culture. British films of the 1920s–40s portrayed a middle-class life with middle-class values in which members of the working

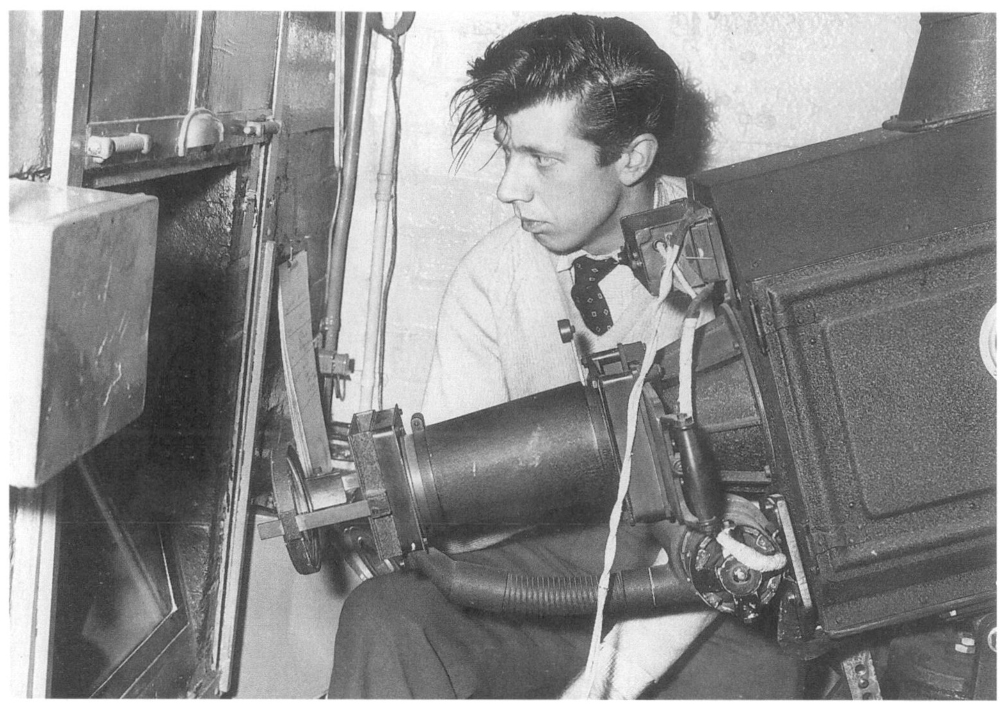

37 Projectionist at the Grand Cinema, Bedford, 1963. (Bedfordshire and Luton Archives and Records Service)

class were often only shown as caricatures. The brasher American films struck a cord with the British working class and young people began to imitate American fashion, speech and music (**37**). Did local popular culture suffer because of this and become the preserve of the elderly? The local historian should consider this, and the reverse process in which some forms of local culture were revived by contact with the outside and the middle class.

Radio also promoted middle-class accents and values, and these had permeated into almost every home by 1932 when most households had a radio. It was difficult to broadcast working-class accents without making the speaker into a caricature or a 'character', and the broadcasts were countrywide so needed to be understood by all. This led to the standardisation of speech known as standard English.

Statistics on the spread of radio can be found in the BBC Yearbooks. These show that by the start of the Second World War only places with bad reception had few households with radios. One way the BBC had of remedying this was to open local transmitters broadcasting local programmes. Improved technology centralised radio broadcasts into regions. The local historian interested in the definition of regions should examine how the BBC divided the country into regions, but should realise that these were not dedicated to producing regional programmes. Local radio stations broadcasting programmes of local interest were not introduced until 1967.

The development of radio introduced a new technology, and new firms specialising in it, which had an effect on the local economy. Marconi of Chelmsford is an example of this.

38 *Television and community 1959. To celebrate the opening of ITV, celebrities were helicoptered into Haverhill, Suffolk as a publicity stunt. (Haverhill Local History Collection)*

They have deposited many of their records in the Essex Record Office. New retail outlets also opened whose existence can be traced through directories and advertisements in the local press, whilst oral evidence and reminiscences will tell the local historian about local listening habits. Amateur radio societies also flourished, and records of their activities can often be found in the local record office.

One of the spin-offs of broadcasting has been the development of smaller and smaller recording equipment, which has helped to encourage oral history. This has led to the formation of the National Sound Archive, which is now part of the British Library, as well as regional sound archives, and the Survey of English Dialects carried out by the University of Leeds. Many local authorities now sell pre-recorded tapes of local residents reminiscing.

The other form of home entertainment that has helped to change social life is television. At first owning a receiver was very rare, which led to shared television viewing. This helped to unite families and neighbours, for example as at the coronation of Queen Elizabeth II. After that television ownership increased with more licences sold and longer transmission hours, and social life began to alter. How did this affect the local community (30).

Socially it began to make each household inward looking, but at first this also helped to make it family-centred. Did this mean businesses such as public houses suffered? Sociological surveys suggest that young people are still likely to find entertainment away from the home and that the decline in some forms of local entertainment such as the live theatre has been matched by the rise of clubs and discos catering for the younger end of the market. Surveys have also shown that television is not an agent for unifying the family as there is much separate viewing, and what is watched depends on the family member's stage in the life cycle.

Radio and television made national sporting events accessible to the whole population. However, despite national leagues and unions professional sport has maintained a local focus, for example as part of a town like Bath and its rugby union team, or St Helens and its rugby league team, section of a city such as Arsenal or Everton, or a county as demonstrated by county cricket. Many of these teams owe their existence to enterprising entrepreneurs observing in the late nineteenth century the commercial potential of the Saturday half-day holiday when workers wanted something to do and would pay to watch good quality games.

Football in its many forms has been played from time immemorial, but cricket was the first be an organised spectator sport. This happened early in the eighteenth century when cricket owed its popularity to the possibilities of gambling on the outcome. County sides started to appear in the mid and late nineteenth century and until 1963 were a mixture of 'gentlemen' amateurs and professional 'players' — terms that indicate the class divide in cricket. The role of sport in class, either within one sport or across different sports, is a fascinating topic which could be investigated at a local level. Equally valuable would be regional studies looking for variations in the types of sport played. These studies would deepen our understanding of society, its values and stereotypes. It could be asked how far does sport now represent a regional culture that was once represented by dialect, dance and custom?

Sport is a doubly important feature of local life because sport, and especially professional team sports, although acting within national leagues, create local tensions that are relieved by the formalised conflict of the match. Furthermore, success adds to local and civic pride and helps to create a feeling of belonging to a locality.

Some professional sports have their own archives, but others have deposited their records in the appropriate record office. The records of the Surrey County Cricket Club are in the Surrey county Record Office, and are typical of county cricket club records. These include minutes, accounts, fixture and membership lists, details and photographs of players and score books. Most county cricket club records will also include plans of the ground and details of its purchase and upkeep, ground staff books and housekeeping books.

Bedford Rugby Club has deposited its records in the Bedfordshire Record Office. The club was founded in 1908 growing out of a team of Royal Army Medical Corps players. Not only is there the usual corpus of documents and ephemera but details of social activities with menus of dinner dances and arrangements for other events, the club constitution, match programmes, and reports from club officials and the club president. Minutes of members' meetings contain information on the election of officers, rules, resignations, correspondence and names put forward for the award of club colours, details of club tie and jersey designs, and information on the club's ground and its buildings.[4]

Tracing the existence of local clubs can be achieved by using the annual handbooks of the sports governing body as the first reference. These are usually available in the central reference library of an area, and should give information on the number of clubs, where they are to be found, and when they were formed. This type of publication may also included lists of participants, the address of the club, which may be arranged county by county, and details of the league in which the club plays. There are also a number of

39 Men v women cricket match, Haverhill Cricket Club, 1931. Men and women played on equal terms, but we do not know who won. (Haverhill Local History Collection)

statistical compilations which the local historian may find of use, for example *Wisden's Cricket Almanac*, and there is also a large amount of data collected by sports councils and federations. The local historian should remember that there are regional organisations of sports such as the Vauxhall League in football as well as places central to each sport like Twickenham, Wembley or Wimbledon.

Many local historians are likely to concentrate on local teams who play on the village green or recreation ground (**39**). Participation sports of this nature also have governing bodies and sports yearbooks that show when and where amateur clubs flourished. A sizeable number of these clubs have deposited their records with the appropriate county record office, or local studies library.

Village cricket clubs have a variety of records. These include fixture lists and results, minutes of the annual general meeting and committee meetings, membership and subscription lists, lists of equipment and details of social events. The local historian will discover when using these records that dances and other forms of entertainment organised by sports clubs were an important part of village life up until the 1960s, as well as being essential fundraising events for the club.

In the 1900s and 1910s the Granta Football Club was the local team of Linton in Cambridgeshire (**40**). Its headquarters was the Sun Hotel, and the strip was black jerseys and white knickers. Its ground was Camping's Meadow, Back Lane. In the winter of 1909–10 it played 21 matches, won 11, lost 6 and drew 4. The next season it played 27, again won 11 of these, but lost 15 and drew 1. Members paid a subscription of 2s 6d a year to belong to the club, and it was an important part of village life.

The Grantchester Football Club records for the 1950s include a list of members and the different classes of subscription they paid depending on whether they were a playing or a

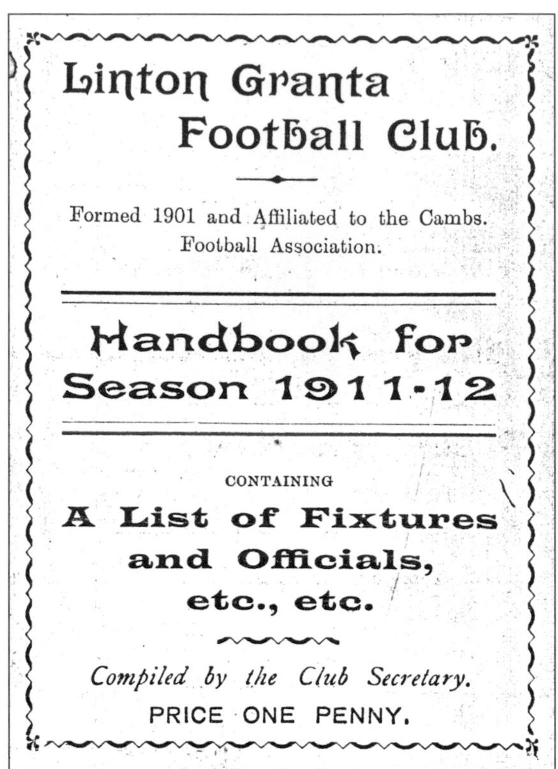
Linton Granta
Football Club.

Formed 1901 and Affiliated to the Cambs.
Football Association.

Handbook for
Season 1911-12

CONTAINING
A List of Fixtures
and Officials,
etc., etc.

Compiled by the Club Secretary.
PRICE ONE PENNY.

40 *Linton Granta Football Club handbook 1911–12. (Cambridgeshire Record Office)*

supporting member. The addresses are given for the members so it is possible to plot their spatial distribution. Playing members came not only from the village but also from Coton, Comberton, Hardwick and Haslingfield (**41**).

They travelled by coach to away games and expenses for this were defrayed by a weekly sweepstake. The club was wound up in 1956, and the local historian could ascertain whether such closures were the result of economic pressure, local demography with a lack of playing members or a fall in interest in the face of other activities. Answering these questions could lead to a better understanding of local society. Perhaps in this case demography played a part as the club re-opened 20 years later when a new generation of players emerged. This time it was short-lived and closed in 1982 when it donated £58 to the Grantchester Youth Centre.[5]

Local amateur football clubs had a number of leagues they could play in. These included the Colts League for juniors and the Sunday League (**42**). In October 1979 the *Cambridge Evening News* reported that the Madingley Rangers Football Club had been barred from the Sunday League and were unlikely ever to be readmitted while its officers were never to be allowed to hold office again because of gross maladministration. The club had been admitted to the league in 1975 but had changed their pitch without notifying the league. On inspection by the league the new pitch had proved to be 'through its unsuitability, a danger to players'. No representatives from Madingley Rangers attended the disciplinary hearings. This might have been a storm in a teacup but it illustrates the tensions between periphery and centre, and a breakdown in communication between the two.

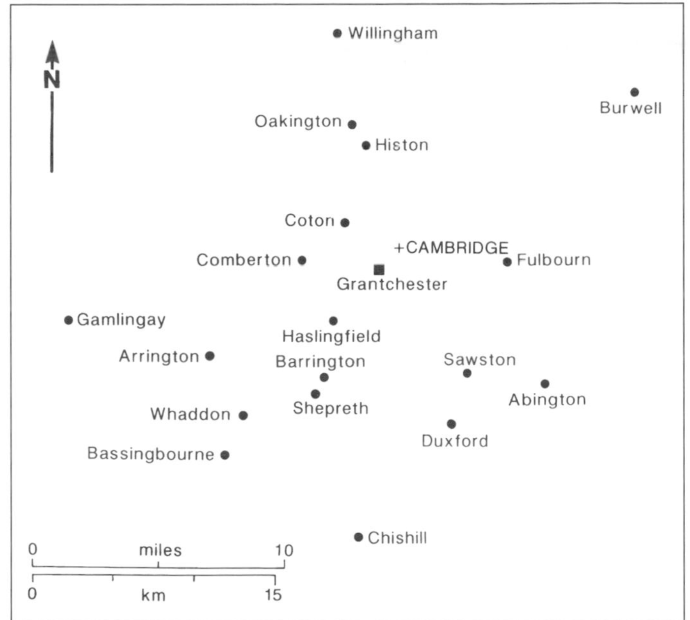

41 *Location of fixtures. Grantchester, Cambridgeshire Football Club, 1950*

42 *St Matthew's Junior School Cambridge, Junior League Champions 1948–49. Although a posed photograph, the pride of these champions is obvious. It marks the beginning of a new photographic technique, which catches the mood of the moment. (Cambridgeshire Collection, Cambridgeshire Education, Libraries and Heritage)*

LINTON TENNIS CLUB.

MRS. HAWKSLEY has very kindly placed her Lawn at the disposal of the Club on Tuesday and Friday in each week. It has therefore been decided to raise the subscription to 3/6 for this season.

TENNIS TOURNAMENT.

A Mixed Doubles Tournament has been decided upon. Entrance Fees:—

Ladies........1/6 Gentlemen........3/-

The Preliminary Rounds and Semi-Finals to be played on Mr. Chalk's Court The Final will be played in Dr. Palmer's Garden, Thursday, August 26th, 1920, on which date it is proposed to hold a Garden Party to raise funds for the purchase of a Tennis Ground.

Partners for the Tournament will be "drawn" for.

Entries close Tuesday, July 27th, 1920

H. TITMARSH.
A. SAMUELS.

43. Linton Lawn Tennis Club, subscriptions and tournament rules, 1920. (Cambridgeshire Record Office)

44 Joe Turner's Dance Band, Haverhill Town Hall, 1920s. The social importance of dance in twentieth-century local life, should not be ignored. (Haverhill Local History Collection)

45 *Half Mile Open Handicap, Cambridge, c.1910. (Cambridgeshire Collection, Cambridgeshire Education, Libraries and Heritage)*

Another local league that encouraged boys to play football was the Colts League, which was usually based on a district centred on a town. Colts Leagues organised knock-out competitions for different age groups. The rules of the Cambridge and District Colts League for 1977 state that 'home teams will provide oranges for both teams'.

One question the local historian interested in sports history might want to answer is whether the footballers played cricket for their home village in the summer, or were the two sports mutually exclusive. Records of village cricket teams will reveal the answer to this. Like amateur football club records these will include membership and subscription lists, as well as minutes and accounts, fixture lists, scorebooks, lists of equipment and details of the pitch, its upkeep and the buildings on it. A comparison of the Grantchester Football Club membership list with that of the Grantchester Cricket Club list of registered players for the early 1950s shows that there were at least six players who played in both teams. However, the fixture list reveals a different pattern to that of the football club and suggests that cricket might have been on a different social plane to that of football.

1959 Fixture List of Grantchester Cricket Club

Plant Breeding Station	Friendly	Melbourn	League
Abington	League	Fulbourn	League
Cicadas	Friendly	Haslingfield	League
Atlas Works	Friendly	Selwyn College	Friendly
Little Shelford	Friendly	Corpus Christi	Friendly
Audley End	League	Kings College	Friendly
Mr Kerridge's Eleven	Friendly	Past Members	Friendly
Trinity High Table	Friendly	The Stags	Friendly
Rodney Drama Eleven	Friendly		

The league mentioned here was League VI South.

The vicar was a member of the cricket club committee, and in 1956 organised a concert for club funds. Other fundraising events included three dances, a jumble sale and a raffle. Earlier in the century Caxton Cricket Club's social agenda had included a cricket supper at the Cross Keys in 1909 and a concert with Morris dancing in 1911.[6]

The social structure of the local tennis club can also be traced through local club records. These should include minutes of annual general and committee meetings, fixture lists, accounts and information about social events (**43**). The records of Melbourne Church Tennis Club cover the period 1930–52. The courts were in the vicarage grounds and the vicar was the chairman of the club, but the club had to pay for the upkeep of the courts and provide their own tennis balls. The membership fees in 1930 were 5s a year for seniors and 2s 6d for juniors. Remarkably these remained stable for the next 20 years. Non-members could use the courts at specified times on the payment of 6d.

One of the main functions of the club was to provide a social life for its members in the winter. Events included whist drives, dances and socials. In April 1934, 75 members and their friends attended a social at which there was a programme of songs and sketches, refreshments and dancing at the end of the evening. Although the membership numbers remained steady it became difficult to find committee members, and fewer and fewer members attended the annual general meetings, and only 20 members attended a dance in March 1941 with music by Joe Cox's Band. Eventually lack of interest and perhaps demographic factors, as young people moved away, led to the club's closure in 1951 (**44**).[7]

Amateur football, cricket and tennis clubs are only three examples of the wealth of sources on local sports clubs (**45**). As we saw in the case of Madingley Rangers a good ground to play on was essential. In rural areas playing fields and recreation grounds were the responsibility of the parish council. The parish council minutes will record the acquisition and maintenance of these and discussion on their use. Parish records will also contain complaints about the state of playing fields and recreation ground as a letter to Linton parish council dated 24 July 1920 shows. The writer of the letter R. Titchmarsh called the state of the ground a disgrace. He wrote that the state of the land made it useless 'except for stump speeches from Labour agitators'. The seats were broken and the cricket pitch had footpaths all over it, while the grass was allowed to grow to over 2ft high in order to assist the man who grazed his cows on it 'to the discomfort of players and spectators'.[8] In towns it was the parks and gardens sub-committees which had responsibility for playing fields and pitches, and deliberations on these will be found in the committee minutes. Sports stadia are sometimes owned by the municipality, and sometimes by a company or club. Before working on these the local historian will have to ascertain whether the stadium is a public amenity funded from public money, or a commercial venture.

Once acknowledged as an integral part of the rural scene, fox, stag and otter hunting are in the late twentieth century areas of great controversy. Nevertheless hunting cannot be ignored, and many are of great antiquity with records going back into the seventeenth century, as for example the Oakley Hunt in Bedfordshire. Some hunts have deposited their records. The Oakley Hunt's records are in the Bedfordshire Record Office. These include tenancy agreements, insurance documents, conveyances of land, agreements made with huntsmen, minutes and correspondence of the hunt committee, subscription lists

46 The Oakley Hunt, Boxing Day, 1909, on St Peter's Green, Bedford. (Bedfordshire and Luton Archives and Records Service)

and point-to-point programmes (**46**). These help the local historian to build up a picture of the hunt's activities, while local newspaper reports will give details of meets, and latterly of disturbances. There are some important questions that need to be asked about the hunt, its supporters and opponents. Is this class based or is it part of the wider tension between town and country, newcomers to the village and natives? Is this really a late twentieth-century phenomenon or did it exist earlier? Has the social composition of the hunt changed or is it the last representative of the landed squirearchy at play? Have relationships with local farmers been affected by the growth of institutions buying land? These are all questions, which although they can be applied to hunting in particular, refer to the wider context of attitudes to localities and local institutions in the twentieth century.[9]

Sport, whether spectator or participation, involves competition in some form, but 'leisure' activities are less competitive and often carried out by the individual in isolation. The Office of Population and Census Statistics carried out a household survey in 1977 that was based on interviews and questionnaires in sample areas. On the question of preferred leisure activities over half of those asked put gardening as their favourite leisure activity. Trips to the countryside and do-it-yourself were also popular and nearly a quarter listed walking as their favourite leisure pursuit. Fishing is also one of the most popular pursuits (**47**).

Records of leisure pursuits such as gardening or do-it-yourself are likely to be commercial, such as the business papers of nurseries, garden centres or do-it-yourself outlets. Personal information may be found in diaries, journals and letters, and of course through oral history. Trade directories will reveal the spread and location of commercial enterprises, but as well as the large national concerns, there are many small specialist

47 *Fishing in the Lode, Reach, Cambridgeshire, 1910. Fishing has always been one of Britain's favourite pastimes. (Cambridgeshire Collection, Cambridgeshire Education, Libraries and Heritage)*

nurseries that advertise in local publications like the parish magazine.

Allotment, floral and horticultural society records have often been deposited with record offices, and will show who belonged to these, when and where their shows were held, what classes there were, and who won the prizes.

Walking could also be organised. The Youth Hostels Association was founded in 1930. National records are at the headquarters in St Albans, but details of local activities will be found in local record depositories. The Ramblers Association and the Kinder Trespass of 1934 highlighted the tension between walkers and landowners, and the underlying tensions between those who use the countryside as a leisure commodity and those who use it to make a living. Again the local historian might wish to examine the social structure of both sides of this, and to ask whether the Kinder Trespass and subsequent protests over access are part of a town versus countryside dispute that is not yet resolved. Swimming in local quarries and rivers is also part of this (**48**).

In 1949 the National Parks and Access to the Countryside Act made more land available for ramblers, but in the late twentieth century there are further tensions as trail and mountain bikes vie for territory with walkers. Overuse of the countryside as an amenity erodes the landscape the rambler wants to admire.

Other leisure activities cater for children and young adults in a formalised environment. Girl Guides and Brownies, Scouts and Cubs, Church Lads Brigade, and the Woodcraft Folk are examples of these. National records are likely to be found in the headquarters of these organisations, but local branches have often given their records to record offices. These may include log books and camp books, details of parades and awards and photographs (**49**).

48 Bathing in the sand-pits at Leighton Buzzard, Bedfordshire. The local historian might reflect on the health and safety implications of this activity. (Bedfordshire and Luton Archives and Records Service)

Other organisations which play an important social and educational role in local life are the Mothers' Union, Women's Institute, and Townswomen's Guild. The local historian can compare programmes and activities of the three organisations and look at their concerns over time, and their role in the local community. Local records are likely to include attendance registers, minutes and accounts. Oral evidence will play a crucial part in reconstructing the place of these organisations in the life of local society.

Other facets of leisure are excursions, trips and holidays. The destination of day trips can be traced through the advertisements of charabanc and coach companies in the local press and their summer timetables which will reveal where they expected the local population to go on holiday (**50**). Some destinations were traditional, for example during holiday fortnight in Leicester, the first two weeks in July, the traditional destination was Skegness.

Details of excursions run by British Railways can be found in PRO AN 25, which are dockets of returns of excursions giving the date and time of the excursion, the number of passengers carried, where they alighted, how much they paid and a report on the weather in the area. For example on Monday 14 May 1951 Excursion Bill A63 Eastern Region 324 passengers were carried on an excursion train from Stratford in East London, stopping at Ilford, Tilbury Town, Greys, Ockenden, Upminster, Romford and Shenfield to Clacton, Frinton and Walton on the Naze. Most, it should be added, alighted at Clacton. The receipts from this were £116 6s and the weather was dull.

During the twentieth century tourism became increasingly important for the local economy. Further evidence for this can be found in resort guides, local newspaper small advertisements, and holiday brochures. Many reference libraries have copies of guides

49 *Scouts at Haverhill, 1911. (Haverhill Local History Collection)*

50 *Charabanc Excursion from Toddington, Bedfordshire to Southend, c.1923. (Bedfordshire and Luton Archives and Records Service)*

covering many years. The local historian also needs to consider the hosts, as not only do tourists boost business, they also change the nature of local society during the tourist season. Tourism means a change in what shops have to offer and services in an area. It means a change in the landscape with caravan and chalet parks, and clogged lanes and streets. Although life cycle tourism has been observed, the local historian could ascertain whether holiday destinations are also class specific as well (**51**).

That we can ask these questions at all shows how accustomed we have become in the

51 *Witchford with Soham Band parade, 1909. Brass band music is popular in all parts of England and Wales. (Cambridgeshire Collection, Cambridgeshire Education, Libraries and Heritage)*

late twentieth century to taking a holiday, and indulging in leisure activities of increasing sophistication. So that the leisure activities in the first half of the century can be compared with those of the later part of the century a case study follows of how one village spent its leisure time in the first decades of the twentieth century.

Case Study: Linton, Cambridgeshire

Linton Parish covered a number of smaller villages, so that in the early years of the century the *Parish Magazine*, one of the sources used to reconstruct the leisure activities of its occupants, covered them as well. The magazine contains valuable information not only on church matters but also on the social life of the parish. However, as with all parish magazines what was included depended on those compiling it, and a change of incumbent or editor can mean a change in the details given. In using parish magazines in general the local historian should remember that they are concerned with the ecclesiastical parish and will reflect parish rather than village or town life. Towards the end of the twentieth century production of parish magazines in some villages has been shared between church and chapel, but again the area covered by the magazine has to be ascertained.

As well as an editorial, parish magazines usually have a homily from the vicar, and may include a list of forthcoming services and the hymns to be sung at them, as well as details of church feasts and special services. The parish magazine should also include details of baptisms, marriages and burials, but again these will only be events held in the parish church and cannot be taken as evidence for the whole village's vital events. The magazine may include details of events and activities held in the parish and news of parishioners

8 o'clock.

The Linton Brass Band

will play for Dancing on

The Cricket Meadow.

9 o'clock.

. . A . .

DISPLAY of ROCKETS ON THE CRICKET MEADOW.

9.30 o'clock.

A

TORCHLIGHT PROCESSION

THROUGH THE TOWN.

10 o'clock.

"God Save the King"

Will be Sung on the Bridge.

LINTON BRASS BAND,

PROGRAMME OF MUSIC.

Mr. G. LINSDELL ... Conductor.

MARCH	"The King's Coronation"	(NEWTON)
FANTASIA	"The Sunbeam"	(RAYNER)
WALTZ	"Waves of Sea"	(MORRIS)
MARCH	"Our Noble King"	(NEWTON)
SELECTION	"Veracity"	(BOURNE)
WALTZ	"Granta"	(Bandmaster LINSDELL)
LANCERS	"Country Cousins"	(BOURNE)
TWO-STEP	"Merrie Men on Parade"	(PECORINI)
FANTASIA	"Diamond Stud"	(GREENWOOD)
BARN DANCE	"Parachute"	(SUTTON)
VALSE	"Felicity"	(HOLLOWAY)
SELECTION	"Welsh Beauties"	(GREENWOOD)
QUADRILLE	"Gretna Green"	(BOURNE)
MARCH	"Minerva"	(CARTER)
VALSE	"Love and Request"	(RAYNER)
FANTASIA	"Olga"	(FRASER)
POLKA	"Lady Ethel"	(FRASER)
MARCH	"Loyal Hearts"	(ANDERSON)

"God Save the King"

52 *Programme of music played by the Linton Brass Band. It is important that the local historian not only collects photographs of bands but also understands the type of music they play. How many of these tunes are still remembered? (Cambridgeshire County Records Office)*

who were away from the parish. In the 1914–18 war Linton *Parish Magazine* recorded details of who enlisted and when, where they were posted, when they were coming home on leave, and sadly, news of their deaths.

The October issue for 1904 has reports on choir outings taken in the summer. Abington Choir's treat was to Clacton where they saw 'General French's forces landing to invade Essex'. They travelled by rail at a cost of £7 17s 6d. Hinxton choir went in the opposite direction from Whittlesford Station to Hunstanton. In Linton itself a day of Old English Games was held with a sale of work in order to raise funds to pay off the churchwardens' debts. In 1905 entertainment laid on in Linton itself included a Magic Lantern show for the Sunday School pupils on St Petersburg and the Russian-Japanese War at the Co-operative Stores with a simpler version laid on for younger children. It is interesting to note that the Sunday School was teaching current affairs as well as religion. The Sunday School prizes were awarded at this gathering. For adults there was an organ recital in the church and an Institute Smoking Concert. Linton Mothers' Union or mothers' meeting as it was more familiarly known had its first meeting in November 1905.

Parish life continued on a fairly even tenor with its annual round of choir outings, Sunday School treats and didactic entertainment until the First World War when the magazine became concerned with the war effort. Peace was celebrated with flags, and the magazine reports that in Balsham an effigy of the Kaiser was burnt. A Peace Tea was held in Linton in 1919 to celebrate the signing of the Treaty of Versailles. Another communal event in which all the surrounding villages took part was a 'Pageant of Christian Worship' held in August 1933 in which each village took a different theme.[10]

53 *Programme of Linton's 41st Annual Flower Show and Sports, 1925. (Cambridegshire County Records Office)*

LINTON.

The 41st Annual

Flower Show & Sports

Official Programme

OF

FLOWER SHOW & SPORTS

TO BE HELD IN THE

LINTON FOOTBALL GROUND

(BY KIND PERMISSION), ON

Saturday, July 14th, 1923.

GATES OPEN 2.30 P.M.

THE

Hadstock "Excelsior" Band will be in attendance

Thurston's Steam Circus

AND OTHER ATTRACTIONS.

DANCING IN THE EVENING.

ADMISSION TO GROUNDS:

2-30 until 6.30 1s. 3d. (including tax). After 6 p.m. 8d.

Children under 12 - 8d.

Secular material on leisure activities in Linton show that there was a full programme of events each year in which many of the villagers were involved. The source for these events are souvenir programmes, posters, and the minutes and accounts of local societies, thoughtfully collected by Dr Palmer and given to the county record office. Dr Palmer was not alone in collecting ephemera about the place in which he lived and many similar collections can be found in record offices and local studies libraries. These show that in the early years of the twentieth century Linton possessed at least two amateur dramatic societies. In December 1904 one gave a concert of songs accompanied by bones, tambourine, and banjo in the National School, while the other performed a programme of sketches, farce and musical entertainment annually. Linton also had a Literary Institute, a Brass Band (**52**) and a Horticultural Society.

The Linton Annual Flower Show and Sports held on the recreation ground was the major event of the village year. The 43rd Annual Flower Show and Sports was held on 23 July 1925 (**53**). As well as the horticultural show and sports there was dancing to the Haverhill Co-operative Society's Band, bowling for the pig and refreshments. The entry fee was 1s which may have deterred some of the poorer villagers from attending, at least officially. Significantly Section I of the Horticultural classes was for 'employed persons only'. The highest prize was 10s for the best allotment.

An earlier programme from 1910 lists the entrants' names. Nominal record linkage with other sources, for example street or trade directories, would reveal more about them.

Linton Tennis Club.

A Garden Party

Held by kind permission
in Dr. Palmer's Garden

On Thursday, August 26th, 1920
AT 2.30 p.m.

Tennis Final at 3 p.m.
Bowling
Concerts at 4.30 and 6 p.m.
Teas at 5 p.m.
Whist Drive at 6.30 p.m.
Distribution of Prizes at 7.30 p.m.
Dancing 8 to 10 p.m.

Admission with Tax .... 2s.4d.
which includes TENNIS
CONCERTS
WHIST DRIVE

Pretty Gardens
Nice Music . .
Good Sport . .

PROCEEDS FOR LINTON TENNIS CLUB.

"EAGLE" PRINTING WORKS, LINTON, CAMBS.

54 *Programme of Linton Lawn Tennis Club garden party, 1920. Note that the admission price includes tax. (Cambridgeshire County Records Office)*

In 1910 some classes were for 'farm labourers only', these included a 'catching the greasy pig blindfolded competition'. Each year there was an inter-village 'tug of war' competition as well as sports which included musical chairs, pillow fights and sack bumping.

On days of national importance the whole village came together, such as at George V's Silver Jubilee on 6 May 1935, and George VI's coronation in 1937. The days included processions, fancy dress competitions, united religious services and teas for the children and the elderly. The important parts of the national ceremony were relayed by wireless through loudspeakers in the recreation ground.

As well as times when the whole village met to celebrate there were social events organised by the various sporting clubs such as the Lawn Tennis Club which played on Mrs Hawkesley's courts on Thursdays and Fridays (**54**). On 26 May 1926 Dr Palmer lent his garden for a club garden party which included a dance in the evening.

Up until the Second World War the village made its own entertainment, but during and after the war the village communal activities started to break down. Better transport and better real wages, especially for the young, made it easier to get to Cambridge and commercial entertainment. More households had their own radios, and later their own television sets so local society became more inward looking. Does this mean the end of village social life? Work by local historians could be directed towards the analysis of village life and leisure in the late twentieth century to see what is organised, by whom, and who joins in. Are we looking at societies which are divided by income, class and cultural aspirations or unified by place?

7 Transport

One of the biggest changes in the life of the local community in the twentieth century has been the transport revolution and the difference that the invention and development of the internal combustion engine has made to the carriage of goods and people. The development of personal transport and the transfer of freight from rail to the road, has dramatically altered the fabric of local society, changing work patterns, employment opportunities and leisure activities.

A fast and efficient transport system, as Adam Smith suggested in the eighteenth century, 'cultivates the remote, reduces prices and breaks monopolies'.[1] Smith noted that canals and navigable rivers were two of the most important forms for the transport of goods. By the late twentieth century although still in use, inland waterways have changed their focus and become leisure areas rather than the arteries of trade described by Smith. At the beginning of the century, however, heavy goods were still being carried by water, and the local historian is in a good position to trace the decline and regeneration of canals and navigable rivers.

A useful reference book which enables the local historian to plot the course of canals and navigations at the beginning of the century is *Bradshaw's Canals and Navigable Rivers* published in 1904, but available in a facsimile reprint.[2] *Bradshaw's* defines navigable rivers as those used for the purpose of trade and describes the different types of vessels found on different types of waterways. It contains an alphabetical gazetteer of inland waterways, which comprises a short description of the waterway, the name and address of its proprietors and its main offices and officers. A distance table between towns is included, the number and position of locks, and where appropriate, tidal information. Details of owners and proprietors are essential for the local historian as these enable the records to be traced.

Railway companies were buying up rival canal concerns. Private owners were either aristocratic colliery owners or the owners of firms such as D. Walker Esq., maltster of Bungay, Norfolk. The sole county council owning a section of canal was Gloucestershire County Council, which owned the Thames-Severn canal from Stroud to Cirencester.

The heavy goods carried in 1904 included coal, cement, iron and bricks, but as *Bradshaw's* pointed out there was no canal clearing house and owners of boats had to deal separately with the management of every waterway used. This fragmentation was partly responsible for the decline of the canal system.

In 1918 the Board of Trade Canal Control Committee issued a handbook on canals which noted that the principal method of transporting goods was by railway, but suggested that the manufacturers of heavy goods should be encouraged to use the waterways. During the 1914–18 war those canals not owned by railway companies had come under government control. In 1918, of the 2500 miles of canals in England and Wales, the railways controlled 1025. *The Board of Trade Handbook*, which should be available in central reference libraries, lists the principal towns served by the canals, the addresses of their branch offices and the types of cargo carried.

The use of canals continued to decline during the first half of the century. A British Transport Commission report describes the condition of the canals in 1955. This describes the route of each canal and whether it was still navigable, making a useful comparison with Bradshaw's list compiled 50 years earlier. The report notes the extent of traffic and tonnage travelling by canal. It points out that although some coal was still carried by canal, the bulk of it was being transported by rail to power stations, while the closure of canal side factories such as at Worcester had caused much hardship to canal boatmen. This is an example of the inter-locking nature of industries in England with the fortunes of one affecting the other.[3]

A British Waterways Board paper published in 1971 shows how within 20 years the whole character of the use of canals had changed to recreational use. The count includes numbers of pleasure boats, walkers, anglers and cyclists, and shows a steady increase in the use of canals for leisure.[4]

In order to trace the records of individual canals the local historian needs to know who the proprietors were and when they owned the canal. The records of canals that were owned by railway companies are in the PRO class RAIL 800-899. Joint stock canal company records are often to be found in the appropriate county record office, or local studies library. Canal company records should include details of directors and share holders, minutes of meetings, correspondence on the running of the canal, toll books, wage books, maps and plans. Further information can be found in quarter sessions records which should include a register of boats and barges using the canal, and an index of deposited plans. See **colour plate 10** for a canal in the 1990s.

River conservators' records can often be found in the borough records of the main borough through which the river passed, or the place where the conservators had their headquarters. For example the Cam Conservators' papers are in the Cambridge Borough Archive held in the Cambridgeshire Record Office. These papers include labour and dredging accounts and ledgers, bank books, and sources dealing with activity on the river such as a toll book of goods passing by boat through Clayhithe and a register of boats on the Cam.

The toll book includes the date a boat passed through Clayhithe, the name of the boat owner, what was being carried and its tonnage. Using toll books the local historian can look at local waterborne traffic and trade. On the Cam 'gaswater' was the main cordage, but there was some seasonal carriage of agricultural and horticultural produce such as chaff, hay, mangolds and potatoes. The tolls show that there was a pronounced seasonal movement of boats with traffic falling off in July but picking up again after harvest. Although the first decade of the twentieth century shows that on the whole industrial traffic on the Cam was brisk, by 1919 there was a steady decline in the amount and the variety of goods carried. At the same time the register of boats shows a great increase in leisure traffic on the river.

The Register of Boats includes the number of the boat, name and address of the owner, the boat's classification, the fee charged and when paid, the amount of a compound lock

55 *Pleasure boats on the Norfolk Broads, 1920s. Still from Beauty Spots of Britain,* The Broads. *(East Anglian Film Archive)*

fee, which could be paid in advance, and remarks as to the fate of the boat, for example 'left these waters'. This type of record enables the local historian to estimate the number of boats on the river for any year, to look at the difference between industrial and leisure traffic and to chart the growth of the leisure industry hiring out boats for pleasure. Figure **55** shows pleasure boats on the Norfolk Broads.

Activities on the Cam make a good case study for the latter, but the pattern can be reproduced wherever there is a river and a large pool of people wanting to use it for leisure. In the 1920s proprietors of boats for hire on the Cam included Mrs Sarah Dolly of Silver Street who hired out punts, canoes, single sculls, rob roys and launches. Down river was the Riverside works which specialised in larger motor launches for holidays, but the bulk of the hired traffic was in central Cambridge where at least 120 punts, 40 canoes and 40-50 other boats were registered by commercial enterprises. Congestion on a fine weekend afternoon must have been intense in the 1920s, and that part of the river is still extremely crowded with punts and other craft today.

Just as the railways took business away from the canals at the beginning of the century, so by the end of the century roads have taken business from the railways. At the start of the century the railways were fragmented into many small companies, but the centralisation and government control of the system during the First World War showed that a more unified system would be more efficient. The 1921 Railways Act combined 27 companies into 'The Big Four' with the intention of including a further 93 companies at a later date. The Big Four were: the Great Western Railway, the London and North Eastern Railway, the London, Midland and Scottish Railway, and the Southern Railway. Companies specific to London were excluded from this act, but were to be included in the

1933 London Passenger Act which created London Transport.

The big four were still private companies, but the idea of nationalisation was mooted in a Labour Party pamphlet in 1939.[5] The Second World War paved the way for this, as did the 1947 Transport Act, which nationalised the railways and created six railway regions: Eastern, London Midland, North Eastern, Scottish, Southern, and Western. The North Eastern and Eastern were later to amalgamate in 1962.

The creation of the regions meant alterations in timetables, but the major effect on local communities followed the British Railways board report on re-shaping British Railways in 1963. This is the infamous 'Beeching Report', and no local historian can ignore the changes it wrought on the lives and landscape of the local community. It is therefore an important source for the local historian.

The report states clearly from the start that its remit is to find a way to make the railways pay. Figures given show that freight traffic made a profit, but many passenger trains although fulfilling a vital social service were running at a loss. This was the area in which Dr (later Lord) Beeching was to wield his axe. Having articulated the general proposals the appendices of the report list the stations and lines to be closed, and details of how the rolling stock released by this would be re-allocated. The aim was to create a dense network of high capacity trains travelling at high speed. Examples are given of costs that would be saved when lines were closed. For example the closure of the 23-mile Thetford to Swaffham line would save nearly £20,000 a year and release a fleet of DMUs for other use.

By comparing the proposed closures with those lines which were actually closed the local historian can identify areas where strong protest groups prevailed. The Reading to Tonbridge line was scheduled for closure to passenger traffic, but has survived until the end of the twentieth century and provides access from Kent to Gatwick airport, and is a valuable artery for rail traffic going to Ashford and the Channel Tunnel. The second part of the report is the maps which show the lines and traffic on them and the proposed closures.[6]

Beeching changed local life and forced people to move onto the roads. The landscape was transformed. Derelict stations and lines in towns became the prey for vandals and decaying eyesores in the countryside (**56**). There was a positive side however, although it took a few years for this to be realised. Railway enthusiasts took over some of the closed lines and revived these as preserved railways. County councils converted others into footpaths and nature reserves, for example the High Peak Trail in Derbyshire, or the Worth Valley in Sussex.

Other sources on railways in the twentieth century can be divided into reference works which are useful tools for the early years of the century, material found in local record offices, which usually includes ephemera such as tickets and timetables, and records in the PRO.

Examples of reference books are *Bradshaw's Railway Guide,* which was published annually, *The Railway Yearbook* or the *Universal Directory of Railway Officials*. The latter gives details of railway and tram companies, and the length of the track they owned for large and small companies. For example from 1925:[7] (**57**)

> Jarrow and District Electronic Railway Co. Ltd.
> 54 miles of track. 4 feet 8 and a half inch gauge.

56 Great Northern Railway derelict warehouses, Derby, 1996

> 10 cars operated by overhead electric transport.
> Chairman and one director based in London, 2 in Gateshead.
> Operation runs from Swinburne Street in East Jarrow.

Material held in local studies libraries and record offices includes local guides to transport, timetables, lists of fares, information on parcel collection, alterations to trains, details of holiday trains, working rosters, signalling plans, route priorities and stabling details, as well as details on staff and wages both before and after nationalisation. Post-nationalisation material includes reports from the new railway companies.

Many areas had their own guides to local transport. In Cambridge there was *Williams Cambridge and District Rail Guide*, published quarterly 1919–49. It includes local advertisements, train and bus timetables, and in the case of trains, fares and times taken. In 1919 the journey from Cambridge to London Kings Cross cost 4s. 7½d. return and took 2 hours 45 minutes on a stopping train, and 1 hour 40 minutes on a fast train. This can be compared with 1999 when a day return to Kings Cross costs £13 50p and a stopping train takes 1 hour 30 minutes, a fast one 50 minutes. In the late twentieth century the trains are faster but there are fewer of them (58).

Details of special trains can also be found. These included Mystery Excursion Trains. A directive to BR staff on the Eastern Region dated 9–15 July 1977 stated on the front:

> The destiny of Mystery Excursions must not be advised to any unauthorised persons, and only BR staff who require the information in the course of their duty.

An example of a mystery excursion, revealed through looking at the working timetable for that week, shows that on 10 July 1977 there was a mystery tour from Loughborough

57 *Jarrow Tram No. 2 turning at Tyne Dock, 1928. (South Tyneside Metropolitan Borough Council)*

heading to Taunton which joined up with another mystery tour from Southend heading to Taunton via Loughborough. The logistics of this trip are considerable and one longs to hear the comments of those from Southend when they pulled into Loughborough. Using working and public timetables the local historian who is also a railway enthusiast can plot the (timetabled) whereabouts of specific locomotives and rolling stock at a given time.

Post-nationalisation, reports such as Anglia's first annual report to its customers published in 1995, come in the form of a glossy brochure. The Anglia report gives details of its fleet, the number of letters received from customers (it does not reveal whether these were complaints), the number of passengers carried, number of services that were less than 10 minutes late, and the number of sandwiches sold by the company.

Records on twentieth-century railways are in the PRO (class RAIL and AN), and include company records, British Railways Board records, maps, plans, timetables, signalling diagrams, staff records and reports on accidents. The National Railway Museum at York has records of rolling stock, and an unsurpassable collection of glass slides and photographs.

Late twentieth-century government policy and environmental concerns might help to revive the railway industry. One cannot be so optimistic about Britain's other great transport industry, shipbuilding, in which it was the world leader at the start of the century, but has negligible output at the end. Like railways, the economy and employment of some towns was inextricably tied up with this single industry, and they suffered accordingly, as have towns connected with docks and seaborne trade.

The rise and fall of shipbuilding and its related industries are both of national and local concern. Those who worked in it, through their reminiscences and memoirs have paid eloquent tribute to the decline of the shipbuilding industry. Economic historians have

S. E. & C. RY. VICTORIA STATION, LONDON.

THREE-POSITION ELECTRIC SIGNALLING INSTALLATION.

BRITISH POWER
RAILWAY SIGNAL
CO., LTD.,
WESTMINSTER,
S.W.1.
Telephone—VICTORIA 2900.
Tel. Address—
"PNEUSIG, PHONE, LONDON."

RAILWAY SIGNAL
ENGINEERS
&
CONTRACTORS

POWER OR MECHANICAL
SIGNALLING.
TRACK CIRCUITS D.C. OR A.C.

58 Signalling equipment, 1925

charted the cyclical rise and fall of the industry, showing that during both world wars the industry was working at full stretch, but this ceased immediately the wars ended. The depression in the industry following the 1914–18 war led to the formation of the National Shipbuilding Security Ltd, which aimed to rationalise the industry and 'sterilised' redundant yards. Palmers of Jarrow was closed by the NSS in 1935 leading to 72 percent unemployment in the town, and the Jarrow March. The industry revived during the Second World War, but again this was followed by a slump. In 1966 the Geddes Report produced more yard changes and as foreign competition grew, British shipbuilders and merchant shipping companies went out of business. The records of the shipbuilding industry reflect the amalgamation of yards in the 1930s. Some records are still in company hands, others can be found in the National Maritime Museums at Greenwich and Liverpool. The records of small yards are often in the county record office, for example records of East Coast barge builders can be found in the Essex and Suffolk Record Offices. Many of the Armstrong Whitworth and Vickers records are in Cambridge University Library and the Modern Records Centre of the University of Warwick also has records of shipbuilders and shipping companies. The most important deposits on the north east shipyards are in the Tyne and Wear Archives in Newcastle.

The types of records referring to shipbuilding follow the course of the ship from its conception to its delivery. The sequence starts with the shipping company asking for tenders and estimates. Each shipbuilding company then prepared a tender, copies of which were kept for reference by the firm. The tender includes design drawings, dimensions, estimates of costs and potential delivery date.

Most companies kept a quotation book, which lists what was to be supplied and to where, with relevant correspondence. Once a tender was accepted a contract was drawn up, and most companies kept a contract book, which contains the date the tender was sent, date accepted, who it was for, what was to be supplied, and when and where it was to be supplied. A list of questions to be asked was appended and a copy of a confirmation of the order was added to the contract.

Yards also kept lists of vessels built by them — yard lists. CUL Vickers PLC 1104 is the register of ships built at the Barrow yard. This includes the order number, the name of the vessel, its dimensions and tonnage, the type of engine and speed, the date of the contract, the expected date of delivery, the date of the launch, the date of the delivery and where the vessel was delivered.

The list of vessels built in the yard shows that by 1902 it was specialising in submarines, and that it had many foreign orders on its books, both for shipping lines and foreign governments, including Argentina, Brazil, Chile, the Imperial Ottoman Government of Turkey, Japan, and Russia. The latter ordered a warship shortly before the Revolution which was not finished until after the Soviets came to power, who would not accept delivery of the ship, so that it had to sold off to the highest bidder by the yard.

Using yard lists the local historian can match expected and actual delivery dates, and estimate the amount of work in each yard on an annual basis. This gives indirect evidence on the local economy and employment. In the case of Vickers, from contract to launch took two years and from launch to delivery one year. The 1960s were especially lean years. The last entry is 1973 when an order for a cruiser HMS *Invincible* was placed.

The local historian can also find information about those working in the shipyards in the company archives. Wages books, safety and welfare books, and apprenticeship registers have often survived.

CUL Vickers PLC 577 is the apprentice records book for Barrow. The firm usually took on about 65 apprentices every year. From 1905–48 entry to the apprentice scheme was by a qualifying examination, after 1948 it was by interview and school reports. Preference was given to the sons of shipyard workers, which added another dimension to the hardship experienced by families in times of depression. An apprentice could start between the ages of 16 and 19, and the apprenticeship was for five years if the lad was aged between 16-18 and until the age of 23 if the lad was 19. The apprenticeship articles included a clause that the apprentice could not join a trade society. Different rates of wages were paid for different crafts. The rates ranged from 5s to 12s a week. The highest rate being for boat-builders for which only two apprentices a year were taken on. Most apprentices were platers or riveters. Vickers also ran a scheme which took apprentices from Argentina, Brazil and Chile. Other company records will include partnership agreements, minutes of meetings and financial papers.[8]

Shipping company records such as Cunard, P&O and White Star are often still in the parent company's archives. The whereabouts of these can be traced through the Lloyds Register of Shipping Records Centre. Information relating to individual ships can be found in the *Lloyds Registry of Ships* or the *Mercantile and Navy Lists of Ships Registered*. Details of the men who worked on the ships are kept in the Board of Trade BT class at the PRO and the National Maritime Museum. The Board of Trade was responsible for issuing certificates of competency and these are also in the PRO. Full merchant sailor service records for 1939–72 with crew lists and agreements are in the Registry General of Shipping and Seamen at Cardiff.

As shipbuilding and the railway industry declined, their place was taken by the motor industry. Motorised travel brought about massive changes to local society and its landscape. New roads, motorways, and car parks have changed the face of town and country, and the accessibility of personal transport has widened the gap between workplace and home.

The compilers of the census were aware by the 1960s of the change in working patterns brought about by the car. The sample census of 1966 included questions on car ownership and asked for details of the means of transport to work, and the distance travelled. Car ownership was concentrated in the wealthier South and South-East. The North-East and Midlands show a significantly lower index of car ownership. The most common way of getting to work in 1966 was by car or train. The figures also show the numbers commuting into a town and those working outside. The difference between the two can be used as a commuting index, and indirect evidence on employment opportunities. Case study towns show that 66 percent of Whitehaven's working population were resident there, and that incomers came mainly from Ennerdale. In Jarrow, 81 percent of the work force lived and worked in the town, and those who did not, lived in the surrounding county Durham.

Table 8 in the 1971 census showed how people travelled to work, and Table 6 divided commuters into socio-economic groups so that it is possible to see who commuted and why. In 1971 skilled workers and junior non-manual (i.e. clerks, typists, secretaries) were most likely to commute, but by 1981 although skilled workers were still prone to commuting, junior and middle management were at the top of the commuting table. The summary returns for the 1981 census shows an increase in the use of the car and a decrease in the use of public transport.

Information on the buses available can be found in a number of sources. Local studies libraries usually have a large selection of bus timetables and routes, which cover from the early years of motorised omnibuses up to the late twentieth century. These can be used to plot the distribution of places served by buses and using a sequence of these enables the local historian to compare these over time.

Local directories are useful for information on bus routes for the early years of the centuries. For example *Kelly's Directory for Suffolk* for 1925 gives the names of bus companies, and where and when they operated:

> Woodbridge [9]
> Ipswich to Ufford. E.W. Cooper's *Bluebird* passes through Woodbridge every hour.
> Eastern Counties, Ipswich to Melton passes through Ipswich every hour.
> Services leave Woodbridge for Framlingham, Saxmundham, and Aldeburgh.

Bus services have always been a mixture of private operators and local authority operated buses. Details of bus services run by local government can be found in the council minutes. Local tram and bus services had to be set up by a private act of parliament, as for example Luton's Electric Tram Service private act of 1907. The text of the act will give information on routes, salaries and fares, and a copy is usually filed in the authority archives. In 1931 Luton Council tried to sell its system to the Eastern Counties National Bus Company, but was prevented from doing so by the Ministry of Transport. Most local authority bus services have corresponding files in the records of the Ministry of Transport in the PRO.

Luton scrapped its trams and replaced these by motor buses in 1937. The records include details of the purchase of buses, monthly returns of route revenues, and mileage travelled.[10] Transport managers' reports are also available, as well as accident or incident reports, and information on ticket machines and uniforms. Financial details of the operation can be found in the local authority treasurer's accounts

The buses themselves were licensed, and details kept on registration cards. These include details of the registration number, the type of bus, its maker, body number, date acquired by the fleet, date withdrawn and whether it was re-numbered when it was withdrawn. The cards, or printed transcripts, of these can be found in county record offices.

Car licence details can help the local historian to identify when cars were licensed and to whom. The registration cards give the type of car and details about its chassis, engine and horsepower. The county council was the licensing authority so car-licensing details will be found in the county council archives. Each county was allocated a set of letters. For example Bedfordshire was given the following sequence:

BM	1-9999	=	1903–21
NM	1-9999	=	1921–27
TM	1-9999	=	1927–32
MJ	1-9999	=	1932–36

In 1936 a prefix was introduced and three-letter numbers were formed in sequence starting with ABM. When YMJ was reached the initial letters were placed after the figure with a letter in front denoting the year of registration. A = 1963 which is the date that the county ceased to register cars.

Information on cars and car ownership is found on registration cards, in a register of licences and in registration files (**59**). These help the local historian to track cars, as re-registrations are added into the register in red ink. The engine and chassis numbers are not entered in the register, but on the cards and in the files.

The register of licences issued in Bedfordshire gives the number of the car, its make, to whom it was registered, and where. By 1960 the information also included the name of the supplier as well as the owner, and blocks of numbers were allocated to local garages. Using this information the local historian can plot garage sale hinterlands. For example in June 1963 the Luton Motor Company registered 12 cars, all Fords, of which six were Cortinas. Three each were sold to buyers in Luton and Bedford, and other purchasers lived in Aylesbury, Bucks., Histon in Cambridgeshire, Kingsbury in north-west London, Rushden in Northants and Gustard Wood in Hertfordshire. In the same month, another garage, this time a Morris dealer also sold 12 cars, six in Luton, four in Hitchen and one a piece in Royston and St Albans. A different pattern of purchases can be seen which leads to questions about the socio-economic background of the purchasers.

Applications to licence a vehicle were filled in on Ministry of Transport form RF8. This form required details of where the vehicle was to be kept, and what it was to be used for. On 1 October 1929 a four-person open dark blue Ford hackney carriage Registration Number BM 9602, with an open body, was registered to a taxi proprietor in Thurleigh, Beds. A great deal of information can be found out about individual cars and their owners by using registration documents.

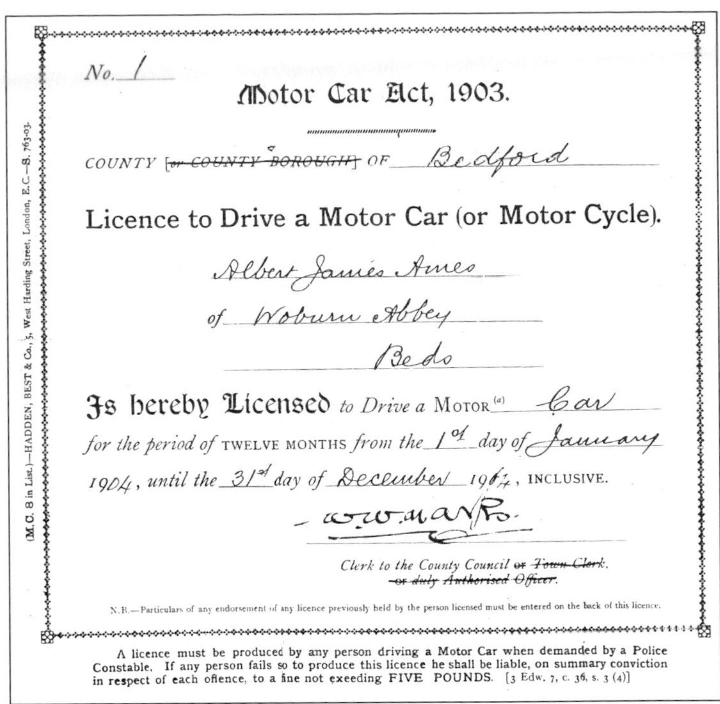

(M.C. 8 in List.)—HADDEN, BEST & Co., 5, West Harding Street, London, E.C.—8. 763-03.

No. 1

Motor Car Act, 1903.

COUNTY ~~[or COUNTY BOROUGH]~~ OF Bedford

Licence to Drive a Motor Car (or Motor Cycle).

Albert James Ames

of Woburn Abbey

Beds

Is hereby Licensed *to Drive a* MOTOR[(a)] Car

for the period of TWELVE MONTHS *from the* 1st *day of* January

1904, *until the* 31st *day of* December 1904, INCLUSIVE.

Clerk to the County Council ~~or Town Clerk,~~
~~or duly Authorised Officer.~~

N.B.—Particulars of any endorsement of any licence previously held by the person licensed must be entered on the back of this licence.

A licence must be produced by any person driving a Motor Car when demanded by a Police Constable. If any person fails so to produce this licence he shall be liable, on summary conviction in respect of each offence, to a fine not exceeding FIVE POUNDS. [3 Edw. 7, c. 36, s. 3 (4)]

59 *First driving licence issued in Bedfordshire, 1904. (Bedfordshire and Luton Archives and Records Service)*

Under the 1903 Licence Survey Act the county council had to make checks of vehicles licensed in registration sub-areas. The information in the Licence Survey Books contains the same registration information as before, but of a more local character. In 1911 a licence survey was taken of the Sharnbrook Registration Sub-District in Bedfordshire. This shows that 130 licences were in use for vehicles scattered through the surrounding villages, but with the preponderance in Sharnbrook and Eaton Socon. Forty licences were for motor cycles, 10 for trade vehicles, and four for public conveyance with the picturesque names including the Ballot at Eaton Socon, and the Mettalurgique at Riseley. The remaining licences were for private cars representing 18 different makes of which the most popular was the Humber.

With the increase of traffic on the roads so the number of traffic offences went up as well. County councils kept a register of motor vehicle offences connected with failure to purchase or renew a licence. The register gives the date of the offence, the name and address of the offender, and registration number of the offending vehicle. It states the date by which the licence had to be renewed, by whom the offence was reported, whether the accused appeared before the benches, any previous offences and the fine levied. A motor vehicle licensing offence could incur up to three months imprisonment, but during the 1950s and '60s most of those found guilty were given a £3 fine. Accidents were frequent from the start of motoring (**60**).

County and borough councils were also responsible for the upkeep of local roads, and were therefore concerned with the amount of wear and tear on these. In order to find out the extent and nature of traffic, local surveys were carried out. These can be found in local authority records in the county record office. County and borough councils usually have

60 *Road accident near Hockcliffe Bedfordshire, 1905. One of the first recorded car crashes. (Bedfordhire and Luton Archives and Records Service)*

a number of committees with responsibility for roads and transport. These will probably include a sub-committee on highways and county roads. The civil engineering department takes on overall control of the upkeep of the roads, and information on the maintenance of car parks, street lighting, numbering and naming, and the position of street signs can usually be found in the records of the Public Works and Town Planning Committee. By-laws on traffic will show how the local authority was responding to changing circumstances. By-laws cover details such as the provision of rear lights on vehicles and riding bicycles on pavements.

In 1901 the Highway sub-committee of Bedford Borough Council took a traffic survey of Bromham Bridge lasting 10 days. The object of this was to decide whether the bridge should be widened. The results of the survey show that 4,043 bicycles used the bridge, 1,947 pedestrians, 1,573 two wheeled horse drawn vehicles, 487 four wheeled horse-drawn vehicles, 2,179 saddled horses and 13 motor cars.

In July 1930 and September and October 1937 Bedfordshire County Council took a traffic census on Watling Street. Each survey was divided into hours and each day's results listed separately. The results for Wednesday are listed below:

Table 22 Traffic Surveys on Watling Street, 1930 and 1937

	1930	**1937**
Motor cycles	313	163
Motor cars	1344	2435
Vans	1034	1457
Buses	169	111
Lorries	188	2546

61 *Early motor oil delivery wagon, c.1910. Part of the increase in traffic on the roads came from vehicles servicing the motor industry. (The British Petroleum Company, plc)*

Tractors	93	30
Traction Engines	25	–
Horse Drawn Vehicles	57	18
Bicycles	343	530
Livestock	9	–
Steam Lorries	18	–
All traffic	3572	7561

This table shows the dramatic increase in motorised traffic over seven years, especially in the use of private cars and lorries, suggesting that transfer from rail to road was well advanced by the late 1930s. The information on the census also makes it possible to compare the amount of traffic on a daily basis.

Table 23 Daily rate of traffic 1930 and 1937

	1930	**1937**
Sunday	4151	7419
Monday	3561	7936
Tuesday	3451	7381
Wednesday	3572	7561
Thursday	3692	7946
Friday	3992	8786
Saturday	3973	10280

62 Hayward's Garage, Haverhill, 1950s. Note the AA motorcycle. (Haverhill Local History Collection)

Once more we can note a dramatic increase in traffic, especially at the weekend. Was this for leisure, or being used for shopping in one of the local towns? The answer to questions such as these will give the local historian information on the spatial and social parameters of the local community, and this would be a case where oral history could play a vital part in filling in the details. Comparison with other traffic surveys and censuses would also be valuable[11](**62**).

Motorways, which have radically altered the landscape, are the responsibility of the Ministry of Transport. Records on the planning of the motorways, the compulsory purchase of land and the construction of the motorway are in the PRO class MT, for example MT 39, 121, 128, 139. MT are the files relating to different sections of motorways, and are useful sources for the landscape historian. For example MT 121/7 is the file for the M6 Preston by-pass section. The file includes a profile of the motorway with plans on which are marked fields and owners' names. A key plan marks points of access and bridges on a large scale OS map noting the motorway's route as it goes through each county. The plan shows how the motorways will alter the fields, and includes the correspondence with relevant county councils (**63**).

Motoring organisations such as the RAC and AA have records dating back to the early twentieth century. Printed sources held at the National Motoring Museum at Beaulieu, and records of the petroleum industry are held at the University of Warwick.

The development of Britain's motor industry can be traced in the Modern Records Archive at the University of Warwick, but there are also deposits in county records offices. Memoirs of working at the Vauxhall factory in Luton are in the Bedfordshire record office. Fodens, the commercial vehicle manufacturers, have deposited their records in the Cheshire Record Office, and other local firms have also placed their records in local record

63 *Sections of the route of the M6 Preston by-pass. (Crown Copyright material in the Public Record Office is reproduced by permission of the Controller of Her Majesty's Stationery Office [PRO MT 121/7])*

offices. Information on the types of jobs offered in the factories can be found in local newspapers, as can advertisements for cars, and details of industrial disputes and other factors affecting the local economy.

Although ideas about the final mode of transport to be discussed have a long history, its development belongs to the twentieth century: air travel. From its tentative beginnings with the armed forces it is now one of the biggest industries, and civil air traffic has

64 Modern BP fuelling unit at Gloucester, 1928. (The British Petroleum Company, plc)

changed the working and leisure lives of the majority of the late twentieth-century population (**64**).

In order to trace airport records the local historian needs to know who owns the airport. Is it managed by the BAA, is it a municipal airport such as Luton, a joint venture such as East Midlands or owned by a profit making company? The records of municipal airports are the easiest to trace as information about their inception and planning will be in the borough or city archives. Information on Luton Airport, for example, can be found in the records of the town clerk's and Borough treasurer's departments. These include plans, acquisition of land and capital expenditure on buildings and equipment. Details of expenditure on salaries, repair and maintenance of the runways, and income. The biggest slice of income came from landing fees, but it took five years before these showed a profit over expenditure.[12]

The noise, loss of farm land and road traffic congestion around airports has led to many local protest groups being formed. Reports about their activities can be found in local newspapers, but many groups have placed their records in county record offices, while the late twentieth-century protests about the extension of Manchester Airport have received wide press and television coverage.

The same is true about road widening and the construction of new roads. The local history of transport protests would make a fruitful area for the local historian to research, and it is a subject with origins that can be traced back to the early twentieth century when farmers complained about motor cars frightening their livestock. Thus it can be seen that, with regards to local society, the developments in transport during the twentieth century have been a mixed blessing.

8 Two World Wars

During the twentieth century Britain has been involved in two world wars and numerous smaller conflicts. War, especially twentieth-century war involves the civilian population as well as those serving in the forces. This is not only through actual contact with the war by air raids but also because special conditions produce special emergency provisions that affect everyone and have an impact on local society.

Many official and unofficial accounts have been written about both world wars, often giving harrowing accounts of the hostilities. This chapter acknowledges the existence of these but seeks to draw to the local historian's attention some of the sources which help to reconstruct the everyday experience of life during times of war.

Historians are fortunate that efforts were made at the end of both wars to collect and assess the survival rate of war records. At the end of the First World War archivists realised that the war had generated an enormous amount of records both official and unofficial. These records were evaluated, and local and national bodies were encouraged to keep rather than destroy them. The multi-volume (British Series) *Economic and Social History of the World War* by the Carnegie Endowment for International Peace included an archival and bibliographical survey of sources on the war.[1] The survey of archives includes a list of local war records and where these were held in 1925, the type of local authority holding them, and its population in 1921. It should be noted by anyone using these invaluable reference tools that many of the sources mentioned are now in the county record office. So that the local historian can understand the range of local records to expect, the return given for Shropshire County Council is reproduced below.[2]

Shropshire County Council

(a) With Clerk of County Council, Shrewsbury. Open to inspection on application.

Information re: Belgian Refugees.

Agricultural Executive Committee (all docs.); appeal tribunal (all docs. at present).

Recruiting Cttee. (minutes, corresp., reports &c).

War Assistance Cttee. (minutes, corresp., accts., case papers, registers, particulars of relief, reports, returns).

National Relief Fund (all docs.).

War Emergency Measures of Council: Education, Police and Special Constables, Public Health, Housing & c., among usual records of council.

List of Shropshire men killed in War (temporarily placed in the Free Library, Shrewsbury).

b) With Clerk to Borough, Urban and Rural District Councils.

Coal Control: Local Military Tribunals; National Registration.

109 Blinco Grove
Hills Rd
Cambridge

Dear Sir.

Roll of Honour

Will you please add to your list the following:-

Eric Golding
3 years.
E. Battery R.H.A.
Bombardier.
22
Single
Before.

Yours faithfully
W. Golding

65 Extract from the Cambridge Roll of Honour. (Cambridgeshire County Record Office, by permission of Cambridge City Council)

c) Forwarded to Headquarters.

Food Control to Div. Food Commissioner, Birmingham, q.v.

Women War Agricultural Cttee. to Min. of Agriculture.

d) Outlying.

War Pensions Cttee., Hospital Training Centres for Disabled Servicemen, at local pensions office, Shrewsbury.

Shropshire Council of the British Legion (including Federation of Discharged Soldiers and Sailors) at United Services Club, Shrewsbury.

War Savings Cttee. (docs. with Assistant Organiser for Herefordshire, Shropshire, and Worcestershire).

Local Red Cross, V.A.D. and St John Ambulance with County Director, Shrewsbury.

Oswestry Boys Club docs. at police Head-quarters, Oswestry.

County Soldiers and Sailors Help Society with local secretary, Overley.

At local offices: Shropshire Produce Co-operative Society, Shrewsbury; Soldiers and Sailors Family Association, Shrewsbury; YMCA, Shrewsbury and Wellington.

Files of local newspapers at their respective offices.

When using contemporary sources on either world war the local historian must remember that censorship was in operation. Vital information may therefore be missing, and some sources were created for propaganda purposes and so must be treated with caution. The counterbalance to these are the factual accounts of local meetings, uncensored diaries, letters and oral reminiscences which can be compared to official accounts of events, and reports in the local and national press. Linking different accounts of the same event may help the local historian to examine in a local context some of the folk myths that have grown up about both world wars.

One of these myths is that of the 'lost generation' killed in the First World War. Regimental casualty lists, war memorials and rolls of honour pay eloquent testimony to their sacrifice, but was a whole generation wiped out by the war? This question has exercised historians for many years. The most authoritative discussion on it is by Jay Winter who suggests that the actual figures for deaths in the First World War are difficult to estimate. However, using the annual reports of the army, navy and air force and figures from the Registrar-General he arrives at the figure of 12.5 percent deaths during the war for the total adult male population.[3] Aggregate figures do not reflect the effect on the local community and Winter shows that not all communities were affected similarly. The summary returns of the 1911 and 1921 censuses show this clearly, but also highlight the problems in using aggregate figures. The summary returns give figures for five-year age bands for males and females divided into counties, boroughs, rural and urban districts. Subtracting the figures for each age group in 1911 plus ten years gives a rough guide to the loss in that age group during the intervening period.

Table 24 Percentage of males aged 10-15 in 1911 remaining in the population aged 20-35 in 1921 for a sample of areas

Accrington	-19
Ashby de la Zouche RDC	-13
Bedford	-26
Birkenhead	+95
Birmingham	+72
Bradford	-8
Exeter	+3
Haverhill	-44
Jarrow	-17
Linton RDC	-25
Middleton	-18
Reigate RDC	-19
Wantage RDC	-81
Whitehaven	-19
Average decrease	-26
Average increase	+89
Mode	19

We can see from this table the wide range in the figures which prompts us to ask how far these figures are connected with the war. Decreases could be connected with adult males leaving to find better employment opportunities elsewhere. The local historian must take

66 *Double military funeral, Caldecot, Cambridgeshire, 1914. W.H. Westcott and W. Nicholas. (Cambridgeshire County Record Office, by permission of Cambridge City Council)*

into account that communities joined the same regiment so that the effect on the local community when their regiment was in action was catastrophic, with whole streets or villages suffering losses at the same time.

Some of these losses can be traced through the rolls of honour kept by local authorities and parish churches. For example Cambridge Borough Council kept a card index of men serving in the forces compiled from information supplied by their relatives. The information on the cards included the name, home address, type of service, particulars of battalion, unit or ship, rank, approximate age, whether married or single and whether enlistment was before or after the outbreak of war. The person giving the information then signed to attest that the card was correct (**65**).[4]

Nominal record linkage between the roll of honour, war memorial or the Commonwealth War Graves database will give further information on the fate of these men. Honouring them however was not the sole purpose of keeping such a list. Another reason was for pension purposes after the war. The vicar of Swaffham Prior in Cambridgeshire not only kept a list of those serving in the forces with their photographs in the church, but was also responsible for checking their pension details and the parish records include details of these.

Parish magazines kept accounts of those who enlisted. *Linton Parish Magazine*, October 1914, price 1d shows that 12 young men enlisted from Whittlesford of whom four were wounded by November and one taken prisoner. Seventeen went from Pampisford and 83 from Linton, 10 from Balsham, 33 from Castle Camps, and 13 from Hildersham. One of those who volunteered from Linton was Charles Day of Vine Cottage, son of Charles and Maria, who lies in the Cemetery of the Four Winds in northern France, having died of his wounds on 10 June 1916 (**colour plate 15**).[5]

67 *Field bakery, Ampthill Road, Bedford, c.1916. Feeding the troops in both world wars is an under-researched area the local historian could investigate. (Bedfordshire and Luton Archives and Records Service)*

The deaths of these young men left unbridgeable gaps in the local community (**66**), but what was life like on the Home Front? War was declared on August Bank Holiday Monday when many firms were closed and their workers away on vacation. Firms placed advertisements in the national press asking them to return and suggesting that they enlist. The early enlistment of skilled men meant that their skills had to be replaced by others. Wages books show that women were employed to do men's jobs in the war, but were often dismissed when the men returned home. Board of Trade reports, the *Labour Gazette*, Ministry of Munitions and Women's Service Committee all attest to the employment of women during the war. After the war the women's sub-committee of the National War Museum, which was to become the Imperial War Museum, started to collect documents about women's war efforts, and sent out circulars asking for reports and literature. The results of their initiative are in the museum's archives. Amongst other occupations women worked as munitions workers, nurses and ambulance drivers and on the land in the Forage Corps which was to become the Land Army.

The war coincided with the fight for women's votes and militant suffragettes. One result of the declaration of the war was noted in the Swaffham Prior Parish Diary. It records that before the war the churches had to be kept locked from fear of arson attacks by suffragettes, but the truce called on the outbreak of war meant that the church could remain open.

When war was declared civilians started to stockpile food, and prices rose dramatically. These are reported in the local press, such as the rise by a halfpenny of loaves sold by the Derby Co-operative Society. In some places, for example Dunstable in Bedfordshire, riots broke out against the higher prices. These civil disturbances would make an interesting

68 Mrs Bradston and the Doms Family, Belgian refugees, Odell, Bedfordshire. (Bedfordshire and Luton Archives and Records Service)

case study for the local historian to pursue and these can be traced through quarter sessions records, police records and the local press. Other targets for rioters were any people suspected of having a German background or name. Related to the latter were the frequent spy scares reported in diaries and reminiscences. An unusual effect on the local community is shown in figure **67**.

In the early stages of the war the local community came face to face with its direct effects as Belgian refugees started to arrive (**68**). A National Committee for Relief in Belgium was set up, which sent out appeals for help to county councils, who re-directed these to parishes. Many parishes responded and set up Belgian Refugee Committees or Belgian Hospitality Committees. The minutes and details of the activities of these committees can be found in parish records held at the county record office.

The Swaffham Prior Committee of Belgian Hospitality held its first meeting in the parish reading room on 1 November 1914. A week later the committee was able to report that many parishioners had made donations and offers of accommodation. A list of accommodation was appended to the minutes. It has to be noted from this that those offering hospitality often stipulated the type of refugee they wanted. Mr and Mrs F of

Partridge Hall Farm Cottage were hoping for two boys. P.C. and Mrs S offered free board and lodging for a child under seven, Mr and Mrs W. board and lodging for a little girl under four with a view to adoption, and Mr A offered free board and lodging for a lad under 17 who would work on the farm.

The first refugees, a family of seven and a married couple arrived in the parish on Christmas Eve 1914. The couple, Joseph and Eugenia de Becker came from Brussels. Joseph, a corporal in the Belgian army had been injured during the retreat. As more refugees arrived, villagers helped to supply clothing and furniture. Although it has been suggested by Arthur Marwick that local communities grew tired of assisting the refugees and the refugees grew tired of accepting charity, local records show otherwise. Refugees moved on not because of pressure from locals but because the early billets in isolated villages did not allow them to work for the war effort. Refugees from Swaffham Prior moved to work in the munitions factory at Letchworth and the De Beckers moved into Cambridge so that Joseph could be closer to his work at Chivers Jam Factory. Many letters of gratitude from refugees can be found in parish records.[6]

The local community also experienced war at first hand from sea bombardments and Zeppelin raids. The first raid was on 19 June 1915 on the Humber and the Thames, followed by many other attacks on civilian targets. The local press has details of these, but reminiscences and diaries help us to understand how the local community felt about these and what local precautions were taken to circumvent attack.

On 31 January, 1915 the parish diary of Swaffham Prior states:

> 'No bright lights to be displayed in the County of Cambridge between sunset and sunrise on account of the fear of bombs dropped from German aircraft (as recently done in Norfolk) so evening service held at 3 o' clock.
>
> 2 April 1915 — In accordance with advice from the Chief Constable a large panel divided diagonally into two with the upper part black fixed to the church tower so that aircraft will know it was a place of worship and will not bomb it, in accordance with the Hague Convention of 1907.'

This was blown down on 13 November 1915.

> '31st October 1915 — Evensong at 3 on stringent orders from the government. No lights to be visible at night. Serious damage was done by Zeppelins on London on October 14th and one of those airships flew over Swaffham Prior, both coming and going at 8 pm and 10.30 pm but dropped no bombs in this neighbourhood.
>
> 31st January 1916 — Six Zeppelins dropped 300 bombs on the North East and Midlands. Killing 54 people. Several were dropped at Isleham, the explosions shaking houses here.'[7]

Government directives show increasing state intervention in local life. This was made possible by the all-encompassing Defence of the Realm Act, known as D.O.R.A. Under this act opening hours for public houses were restricted, munitions workers relocated and food rationed.

Food production became increasingly important as the war progressed. In 1915 County War Agricultural Committees were created. Their records can be found in county council archives. The role of the County WAC was to act as an intermediary between the farmer and the Board of Agriculture with the aim of organising farmers into producing more food. Local branch committees were set up to encourage women and children to work in the fields. When blandishments were found not to work War Agricultural Executive Committees were founded that had compulsory powers. These were also based on the county and had local district committees. The task of the WAEC was to identify under-productive land and bring it into production by giving the farmer equipment, labour, seed and fertilisers. If this did not work the committee had the power to take the land into its own hands.

In March 1916 the War Agricultural Committee of the War Office asked the county and district committees to supply statistics of the acreage in production. The survey was taken by sending each farmer a form on which they were asked to give details of acreage under arable, orchard, market gardens, and pasture. The state of the land was to be classified as 'well-done', 'indifferently done' or 'derelict'. These forms have a low survival rate, but those which have survived will be in the county record office and they provide an invaluable account of land usage in the second decade of the twentieth century. In counties where labour was in short supply a labour census was taken as well. Once this was compiled the Food Production Department organised rotas of equipment and allocated labour as it was needed. This included POWs, the Land Army, conscientious objectors and schoolchildren. All were paid a living wage and camps were established in harvest time for townspeople.

Records of the war agricultural committees include the minutes of meetings, horse permit books, accounts of credit given to farmers, and the use of POW labour. The Cambridgeshire Agricultural Executive Committee records include exemptions given to soldiers during harvest and help extended to small holders. This included credit given to smallholders in Gamlingay when their land was sold after the death of their landlord.

From the minutes of the committee it can be seen that breaking up grassland for cultivation brought with it problems and an outbreak of wire worm. Farmers had to apply to the committee when they wanted to plant a crop such as mustard. The minutes also include details of ploughing and harvesting operations and the classification of POWs into good workers, indifferent, and idle. They were paid according to their classification.

The work of the committees continued after the war when they provided training in agriculture for ex-servicemen, supervised the return to grassland of newly-ploughed land and estimated the amount of compensation to be paid to farmers who lost land to the war effort. This included land lost to new aerodromes, such as at Duxford and Fowlmere in Cambridgeshire.[8]

Another task at the end of the war was to find a suitable memorial for the men who died. As many of these had no known graves, or were buried overseas, a war memorial became a focus for the mourner, and an important local landmark. This was the first time that the civilian population had been involved in such memorials as usually this was left to the regiments. War memorial committees were organised by local authorities, but were not official, and the members of the committees consisted of a mixture of councillors and interested parties. Despite their unofficial nature the war memorial committee records are usually found in the local authority records (**69**). These will include minutes of discussion

69 Unveiling the Coates memorial, April 1920. (Cambridgeshire County Record Office, by permission of Cambridge City Council)

on the form the memorial should take, and deliberations as to whether it should be a practical or ornamental monument. Once this was decided debate followed on what it should look like. Many committees put the design of their memorials out to competition, and the records may include the losing designs as well as the winner. Building the memorial was open to tender and estimates of costs and materials will be found in the committee records. As the memorials were funded by public donations there should be a list of subscribers, and evidence shows that in some places grand ideas had to be reduced when funds were not forthcoming.

Swaffham Prior's war memorial committee decided on a most unusual memorial which was unveiled on 21 December 1919. This took the form of a window in St Cyriac's church. On the window was a sacrificial cross with a Zeppelin at the top, and including a German submarine, a tank and a Red Cross nurse tending soldiers. The vicar recorded in the parish diary that the *Morning Post* described the window as 'unusual' and the *Daily Sketch* as 'bad taste'.[9]

Local records and reminiscences show that celebrations on Armistice Day were muted, and it was not until the signing of the Treaty of Versailles that people really believed that the war was over. Once the treaty was signed there were celebration teas and parish feasts (**70**).

There are a great variety of sources on the Second World War accessible to the local historian. The main problem is selecting which to use. There are oral and printed reminiscences of civilian life in the war. There are official and unofficial accounts, national and local records as well as a vast number of books and pamphlets on the war. This section discusses some of the official and semi-official sources that exist, but ends with the

70 *Peace celebrations. Dinner on Parker's Piece, Cambridge, 19 July 1919. (Cambridgeshire County Record Office, by permission of Cambridge City Council)*

intensely personal diaries kept for Mass Observation.

Alerted by events in the Spanish Civil War the government approached the outbreak of the Second World War with plans already in place for the evacuation of children from target areas. The Committee on Evacuation reports in the PRO INF 1/292 show that local authorities were told to canvas for billeting, and that parents in vulnerable areas were sent a circular asking if they were willing for their children to be evacuated in the event of war.[10] Figure **71** shows evacuees arriving in Bedford shortly after war was declared.

Civil Defence and War Emergency Committees were set up by local authorities to co-ordinate events. Local surveys printed during and after the war perpetuate the myth that evacuees were verminous bed-wetters. Those writing the surveys were middle class, while the bulk of the evacuees were working class, often from deprived areas. 'One surprising experience which seems to have been found all over the country was the large number of children found to be bed-wetters', wrote two members of staff from Westmoreland County Council. The Cambridge Survey of Evacuation contradicts this noting 'no verminous children and only one bed-wetter'. The Cambridge Survey describes the arrival of trainloads of children and their transportation to dispersal centres. The organisation was the result of co-operation between the voluntary services and the Evacuation Sub-Committee of the Borough Council's War Emergency Committee. Minutes of the committee show that there were 2,120 unaccompanied child evacuees in the town by January 1940. Some of these had returned home by March of that year but bombing of London in September 1940 led to further evacuation. This time the Evacuation Sub-Committee had more difficulty in finding billets. In August 1944 there was a peak of evacuation into Cambridge when 5,000 flocked to the town.

The Blitz itself is well-documented in print, film and oral history. Local protection from

71 *Evacuees arrive in Bedford 5 September 1939. (Bedfordshire and Luton Archives and Records Service)*

air raids was made through the local authority's air raid precaution committee which organised the erection of shelters, air-raid posts, and arranged emergency accommodation and medical services. Minutes of the air raid precaution committees should include details of enemy raids and casualties, the location of shelters and how these were administered. The WVS played an important part in this. Records of their activities can be found in monthly reports made to the local authority.[11] An ARP procession is shown in figure **72**.

County councils set up their air raid precautions committees between 1937 and 1938 after the passing of the 1937 Air Raid Precautions Act. At first the chief constable recruited wardens but in 1938 responsibility was given to the chief clerk of the county council who had set up first aid posts, organised training of the warden and carried out blackout exercises. The chief clerk of the county council also kept records of raids.

One of the warden's duties was the recognition of gas. Local authorities produced pamphlets on different types of gas, and on aircraft recognition, which can be found in record offices and local studies libraries, as can the incident cards issued to wardens. Information on these included the street, names of occupants and details of the incident.

A feature of the air raids which has received little attention is the fate of pets in bombed-out areas. This was one of the concerns of a Mass Observation diarist living in Wellow near to Bath. She describes the raid on Bath of 11 June 1942. When it was over the local vet set out to help the city's animals, whilst the PDSA set up emergency clinics. Some of the bombed-out animals were taken back to Wellow to convalesce and the diarist looked after and rehabilitated a Sealyham called Peter.

Anyone who has watched *Dad's Army* will know that the great rival to the ARP wardens

72 *Wartime procession, Castle Ward, Bedford ARP, c.1940. (Bedfordshire and Luton Archives and Records Service)*

was the Home Guard. It was set up as the Local Defence Volunteers after a speech by Antony Eden on 14 May 1940 in which he appealed for a citizen's army. The Home Guard, as it eventually became known, deliberately set out to be a 'paperless army'. Thus its records are relatively sparse. There are however reminiscences and books on local Home Guard units which make a good starting point (**73**).

The Home Guard was raised by the Territorial Army Association through county and regional headquarters, so some details will be found in their records. These include details of officers which were entered in the company record roll, and monthly returns on each platoon's strength. Other records can be found in the Imperial War Museum and the PRO, including PREM 3/223/3 files which include letters from the Prime Minister on whether the rank and file should be called 'volunteers' or 'privates', and the type of cap badge which should be issued. Also included in this class are aggregate returns on the numbers of men enlisted, their weapons and equipment. These include weekly returns are divided into area commands.

Information on what was expected of the Home Guard can be found in *The Conditions of Service in the Home Guard*, 1942, and War Office Regulations, 1943. These show that the expected training and duty period was 48 hours in every four weeks, and that the local Ministry of Labour was to be notified of all enrolments, which created another source on the men who served in the guard. An unusual fact which emerges from these publications is the Home Guard Pigeon Service. Chief signal officers were to be issued with pigeon equipment and to appoint pigeon supply officers (PSOs). They were to be given National Service Pigeon Lofts (NSPLs). If the birds were engaged on 48 hours active service they were to be supplied with pigeon food.[12]

More plentiful at a local level are the records of the parish invasion committees, which

73 *Home Guard parade, Bedford High Street, 1942. (Bedfordshire and Luton Archives and Records Service)*

are usually to found in county record offices classified with other parish documents. These committees were set up after Dunkirk in 1940, and provide an under-used glimpse of parish life during the war. The committees were co-ordinated by the regional defence committees and worked in co-operation with the local ARP. The government issued each parish with guidelines on how to organise themselves and booklets on defence. Examples of these can be found in local studies libraries, such as the series of Public Information Leaflets on 'masking your windows' and another on the same subject 'mother keep it dark'.

Parish invasion committee minutes include committee membership lists, reports on exercises, and bulletins issued to householders on where to go for supplies in the event of an invasion. Girton Parish Invasion Committee held an exercise on 29 May 1942 that exposed its weaknesses. The report notes that messages were duplicated and fire fighters wrongly directed. By 2 June, however, the committee were relaxed enough to organise a Garden Party.[13] The parish invasion committees were disbanded in autumn 1944. Perhaps more than the Home Guard, which was for adult males only, the invasion committees involved the whole community and their records make a valuable contribution to the life of the local community in the Second World War.

Other committees and organisations which impinged on local life were the food control committee, and the fire auxiliary service. Records of these can be found in local authority files. These may also include lists of casualties and those made homeless, lists of schools evacuated, details of warden posts and cleansing stations.

As the extent of the bomb damage became clear one of the concerns of national and local government was reconstruction. In order to find out what the public wanted for the future, local authorities either took their own surveys or commissioned these from Mass Observation. The results of the surveys and plans for reconstruction can be seen in printed

74 *Hobart Road, Cambridge, decorated to welcome home prisoners of war, 1945. (Cambridge Collection, Cambridgeshire Libraries, Education and Heritage)*

form, or in the Mass Observation Archive, in the minutes and papers of the town planning committee or engineers department of the local authority. These will include plans and maps as well as details of the survey and discussion on the types of housing to be provided. Peace celebrations are shown in figure **74**.

One of the most poignant echoes of the war can be found in the diaries kept for Mass Observation by 500 ordinary people. Of course not every diarist was punctilious in keeping a daily account, and the amount of detail given varies. Some diaries are accounts of everyday events such as shopping and cooking, others reveal the innermost emotions of the writer, and demonstrate how these were changed by the war. One of these was a correspondent in a northern town aged 30 when the she started the diary in 1939, married with two children and a husband in the army. She worked in a first aid unit.

C, as we will call her, was unhappily married and in love with a man she had met at the first aid post:

> Jan 10th 1940 The day of days. Seeing B.W. at 9.45pm Got thro' the day somehow or other. Finished work at 2 pm, go straight home. At least I can have the weekend to myself, as O. (husband) can't possibly get off this week, surely! Girls have to sleep. Leave them tucked up & cosy in bed and go out at 9.45. Not 5 minutes walk from home on hill-top with B.W. Can't ask for anything else in life than to be with him. Talk it over and come to the conclusion we shall not wait any longer than we can help, but that means at least 5 years, I wonder if we shall do it.

While she was on the hill the local gasworks was hit and she came close to running home

75 Wreath laying at Castle Camps. To show we will not forget. (Haverhill Local History Collection)

to her children. Her husband came home for a few hours the next day. 'Forces himself on me, and then apologises for his failure (You asked for it M.O.) I hate and loathe him.'

Obviously an attractive woman she goes out with other men, but cannot overcome her love for B.W. At one point her husband rapes, and ill-treats her and then forces her to destroy the dog she had adopted. She considers leaving him or committing suicide, but eventually she suffers a mental breakdown. Nevertheless C was a survivor and kept her diary going with gaps up to the end of the war. In her case the diary acted as a psychotherapist into which she could pour her longings for love and affection.

Undoubtedly the war gave C more freedom than she had before, and the opportunity to compare her life with that of others. We can compare this with the diary kept by U who lived near Bath: 'June 10th 1942. I think neighbours have found life more interesting than me since the war especially childless women who are looking after evacuees.' Ten days later her life had changed: 'June 20th 1942 Great surprise today an air force officer has been round the village getting accommodation for his men. I offered to take two.' The diary barely conceals her delight in these two young airmen, although she is worried how she will feed them. She notes 'they are just like schoolboys'.

Other resources in the Mass Observation Archive enable the local historian to ask specific questions, for example about the behaviour of evacuees. Using these records with local and national newspaper reports, oral accounts and official documents, the local historian can build up a picture of life in a local community under stress (**75**). We will remember them.

9 The countryside

From George Bourne in 1912 to John Connell writing at the end of the 1970s the twentieth-century countryside has been recognised as an area in flux. Land and houses pass to new owners who have new expectations as to what the countryside should offer.[1] Change has produced tensions as rural England is a complex place with different sections of society having different perceptions as to what it means.[2] The local historian can examine these changes minutely and put them into the context of wider change.

One of the most useful tools for the local historian working on change in the countryside will be maps. Ideally one should start with the most up-to-date version of an Ordnance Survey map and work backwards, peeling off additions until the original landscape is revealed.

O.S. Map Scales

1:250,000 = 1in. to 4 miles. Routemaster series. Regional scope, for example South East England covers an area from Bournemouth to Birmingham to Great Yarmouth to Hastings.

1:50,000 or 1¼in to 1 mile. Landranger series. Smaller regions. For example sheet 187 Weybridge to Croydon to Horsted Keynes to Horsham.

1:25000 or 2½ in. to 1 mile. To cover the same area as sheet 187 would need 14 different maps. Detail shown includes settlements, houses, roads, fields, farms, commons, footpaths, historical and archaeological monuments.

Major revisions of this series took place 1903–13, 1940–7, 1952–73.

All of the above maps can be purchased commercially, but for larger-scale maps the local historian is better off using a record office or local studies library. Larger-scale maps include:

1:10,000 or 6in to 1 mile. Revised on a 20-year continuous cycle.

1:2500 or 25in to 1 mile shows roads, boundaries and buildings to accurate scale.

1:1250 50in to 1 mile series produced only for major towns and urban areas. Published from 1945 onwards.

Time series of maps such as the *A-Z* guides produced at regular intervals will show physical changes on the periphery of towns as will town and village guides, and descriptions in trade and post office directories. The Post Office itself produces maps of postal regions which are available at the Post Office Archives (see **colour plate 16**).

Features in the countryside that the local historian should be looking for include the existence of new buildings and roads, the disappearance of railways and change of use in farming land. Motorways in particular have dramatically changed the landscape in some areas.

Two other series of maps have information on land use. The first series is connected with the valuation records pertaining to the 1910 Finance Act. The valuation books have already been discussed in connection with housing. But as well as an entry in a valuation book, details of each property were transferred onto plans based on OS maps. Working plans are found in the county record office, and the finished plan in the PRO. Also in the PRO are the Field Books, PRO IR 58. The key to IR 58 is found in the final plan which gives the valuation district, area and assessment number. IR 58 contains details of each farm in an area including: situation, description, extent, occupier, owner, interests, e.g. freehold, leasehold, tenancy term, length and how much left, how determinable, rent, any other charges, outgoings, e.g. land tax and who paid by, tithes, who pays rates, taxes and insurance, who is liable for repairs, fixed charges, former sales, road and access, particulars of the farm and description, dimensions of buildings, and valuation and anything affecting this, such as buildings in bad repair. IR 58/69667 is the field book entry for Braes Farm in Nutfield, Surrey, a freehold farm occupied by F.B., owned by Mrs F. and let on a yearly tenancy of £198 12s. The farmhouse was well built of brick and was partly weather boarded with a tiled roof. The ground floor consisted of a tiled hall, two sitting rooms, an office and brick entrance, kitchen, large scullery, pantry and cellar. On the first floor a passage led to three bedrooms, two dressing rooms, bathroom and box room, on the second floor were three attics. Water was supplied by a well. On the farm were four old cottages of brick, stone and tile. The land was crossed by a public footpath, and the valuation was £5500.

Houses and shops were also described in the field books such as this entry for Gamlingay IR 58/16547:

> Mill Street — House and shop owned by G.B. of Potton, Beds, occupied by F.T. at a rent of £9 10s p.a. A brick slated structure comprising a small shop, entrance hall, sitting room, kitchen, 3 bedrooms. Rather poor yard at back with brick tiled and stone loft over brick wash house, small garden, brick and tiled earth closet. The outbuildings are in poor repair.

The local historian will find the sources produced by the 1910 Finance Act of inestimable value for projects which range from a history of a house to a larger-scale project on owner-occupation, regional building styles, or comparisons of rent.

Another set of maps of the countryside were produced during the Second World War as a result of an investigation to find out the amount of cultivatable land available and how it could be used. In order to gather this information a survey was taken by the County War Agricultural Executive Committees with the purpose of classifying farms according to their efficiency of output related to the fertility of the land. Farms were classified as A, B, or C, and those in the lowest category C could be taken over by the War Agricultural Committee. Only the smallest holdings under 3 acres were omitted from this survey. Between 1941–3 the farmers themselves were asked to supply further

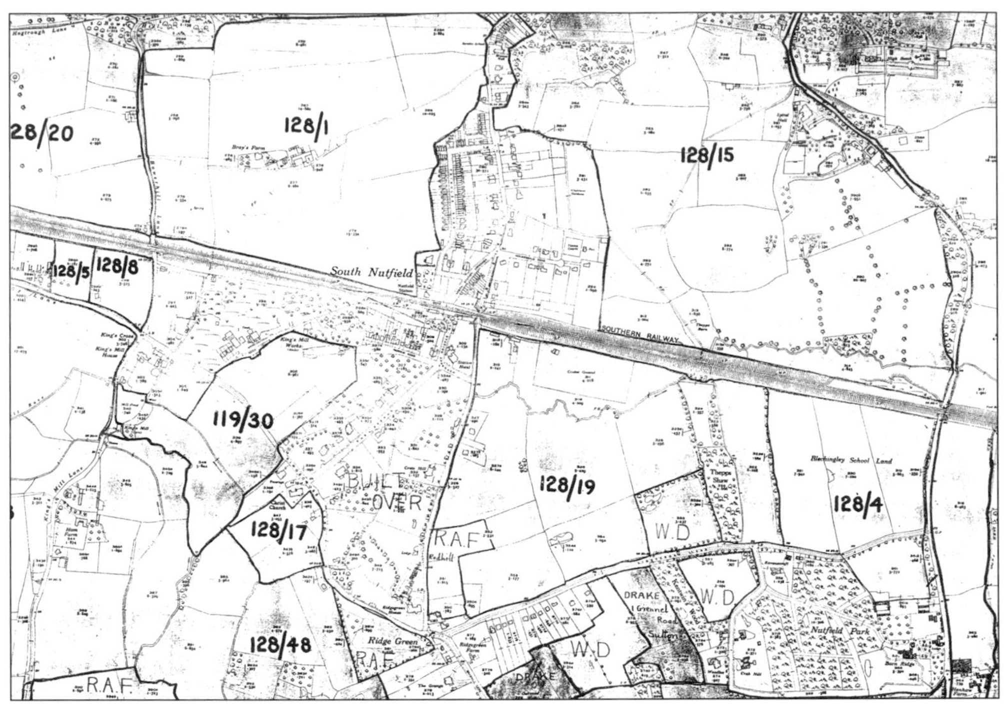

76 The national farm survey map of Nutfield MAF 73/40 No.35. (Public Record Office)

information on forms sent to them for the purpose. The whole is known as the National Farm Survey, and the documents and maps are in the PRO. See for example the map for Nutfield (**76**).

The forms are found in MAF 32 which is arranged by county, and within the county by parish. If you are not sure in which parish the farm lies, the key is in MAF 73 — the maps produced for the survey using 25in and 11in OS maps. This has an index volume MAF 73/64, which is arranged in county sheets with a superimposed grid that enables each farm to be traced.

Each parish file of MAF 32 contains three sets of forms. Form B496/E.1 contains the basic information on the farm, as supplied by members of the War Agricultural Executive Committee: its address, county, district, parish and OS map reference, tenure and owner, the status of the farmer, whether full or part time or a 'hobby' farmer, and if part time the nature of the other occupation. It also states whether the farmer has other land. Questions asked on the form concern the nature of the soil, whether it was heavy, medium, light or peaty, the situation of the farm with regard to access from road and railway, the condition of the farmhouses, buildings, fences, ditches and field drains, and the number and conditions of cottages belonging to the farm.

Arable and grazing are described. The second form (C51/554) asked the farmer for information on crops, and the third (C47.5.5.4) for details on labour, the number of tractors on the farm, rent and length of occupancy.

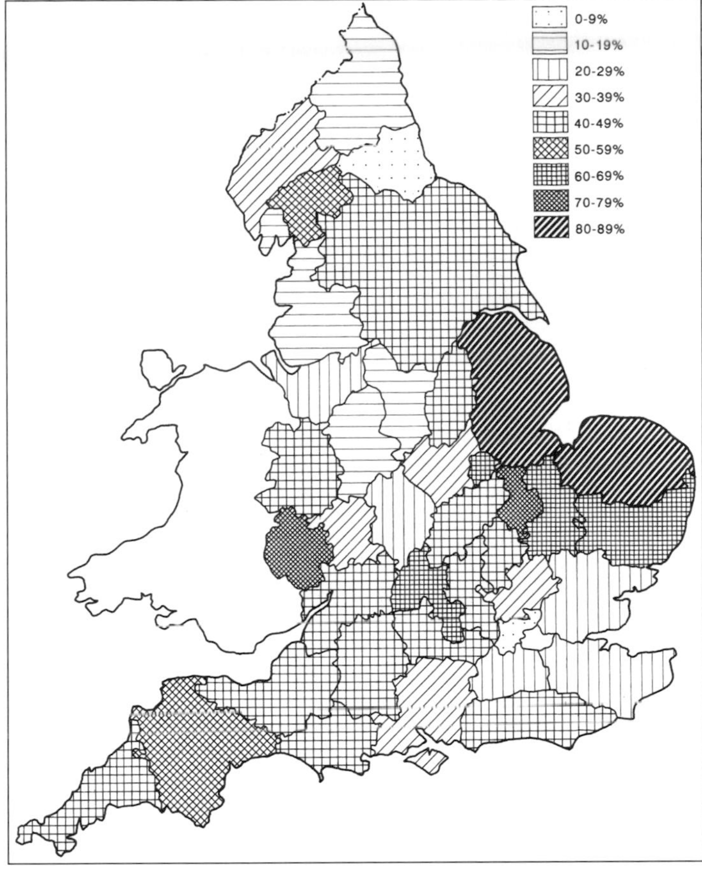

77 *County distribution of agricultural workers in 1901*

The problem in using the forms is that the War Agricultural Committees were asked to make value judgements on the condition of the farm and how they perceived its efficiency. These decisions were not without bias and often the classification given to the farm does not always relate to the judgement on the condition of the land and crops. Nationally only five percent of farms were placed in the lowest category, but there were and are sensitive issues in this. When using these documents the local historian must exercise great care to preserve the anonymity of the farmer and to handle any confidential information in a way that will not give offence or hurt either the farmers or their relatives.

One useful way in which the National Farm Survey can be used is as a comparison with the 1910 field books. MAF 32/1050/128 is for Braes Farm, Nutfield. From this we learn that the farm was 65½ acres, growing corn, potatoes, turnips and mangolds, but mainly put down to grass with 22 acres of mowing grass and 20 of grazing grass. Livestock included 24 cows, 41 pigs, and 220 fowls. The farm had changed hands two years earlier with the new tenant paying an annual rent of £150. The farm was judged to be well laid out. However, the farm roads, fences and ditches were in poor condition, although the field drainage and the two remaining farm cottages were in good repair. The arable was described as fair and the pasture as good, but despite this it was given a low classification with the general comment that the farm had been well farmed by the previous tenant but

78 *Celery picking, Burnt Fen, 1941. (Cambridge Collection, Cambridgeshire Libraries, Education and Heritage)*

79 *Celery planting, Burnt Fen, 1941. (Cambridge Collection, Cambridgeshire Libraries, Education and Heritage)*

was being farmed out, with too much specialisation of pigs and potatoes while the dairy side was under stocked.

Perhaps because of the sensitive nature of the information given in MAF 32 it is better for the local historian to use it for projects with a wider and more general scope than the examination of a single farm. MAF 32/811/82 for Gamlingay which was a late enclosure area shows that the average farm acreage was 6 acres, and that tenant farmers held land from a number of owners in different locations which reflect the older strip field system. For example, R.C. of Church Street held 3½ acres from one owner and a further 23 from Downing College, Cambridge. The committee commented that the farm was not conveniently laid out as the land was dotted around the village. R.C had farmed it with the help of his family and casual labour for eight years. In Gamlingay we can see the last vestiges of peasant farms and the National Farm Survey makes it possible for the local historian to trace the distribution of small family-run farms within a county or a region. The national farm survey can be used in conjunction with the Land Utilisation Survey taken in 1942 and published as *This Land of Britain*.

Further information on who owns the land can be found in the register of land purchases kept by county councils following provisions in the 1959 Town and Country Planning Act and the 1961 Land Compensation Act. This gives a short description of the property and the purpose of its acquisition.

The prime function of the countryside is agriculture and the production of food. Over the twentieth century this industry has seen massive changes. Once the countryside was a main employer, but at the end of the century only two percent of the total adult workforce is involved in agriculture. The map **(77)** shows the situation in 1901.

The numbers employed in agriculture depend to a certain extent on the type of farming in an area, and the type of farming also has an impact on the local landscape. Information on this can be found in PRO MAF 68, which are the parish summaries of agricultural returns, an annual collection of agricultural statistics, which the Board of Trade started to collect in 1866 and transferred to the Board of Agriculture in 1889. The returns were voluntary until 1917 when they became compulsory. As well as the annual parish summaries in 1966 a centennial volume was produced, which makes a good starting point for the local historian and should be available in the local reference library.

The parish summaries are classified by county and then by parish. The information given for each parish includes the number of farmers and size of farms, relative acreage of crops and grass, and number of livestock. It should be noted that there were some changes in the information supplied, different questions were asked, and the scale of measurement changed from acres to hectares. However, the parish summaries give valuable time series information on farming for any given area, or a snapshot of an area for any chosen year of block of years. The parish summaries have a 35-year closure on them. Fen farming is shown in figs **78-9**.

Gamlingay in 1903 (MAF 68/1999)

77 farmers of whom three quarters farmed less than 50 acres. Ten percent of the farms were owner-occupied, the rest were tenant farmers. Of the 3,306 acres, wheat, barley, oats and rye took up 18 percent, peas, beans and root crops 23 percent and the rest was grass.

There were 185 cattle, 429 sheep and 311 pigs on the farms.

Linton in 1903 (MAF 68/1999)
26 farmers of whom 10 farmed over 50 acres. Thirteen percent of the farms were owner-occupied and the rest rented. Of the 7,190 acres 72 percent were arable, but the large number of sheep in the area suggests that these were fed by the turnips, mangolds and kohl rabi grown in the parish.

Nutfield in 1903 (MAF 68/2028)
31 farmers, half of whom farmed 50-300 acres. Fourteen percent were owner-occupied and of the 3,617 acres 28 percent were arable and the rest was grass given over mainly to cattle and sheep.

A longitudinal survey of Nutfield shows how the agriculture changed, In 1923, MAF 68/3153 shows there were only 25 farmers, but 28 percent were owner-occupiers. The average farm size was smaller, with half the farmers farming less than 20 acres (the size bands had changed by 1923). Arable accounted for 27 percent of the acreage, but the number of sheep had fallen to 21. By 1923 labour statistics were also given. There were 67 full-time male farm workers and six female in the parish, 12 male casual workers and five female. In 1943 (MAF 68/3153) the number of farmers is not given, but this can be ascertained from the National Farm Survey as being 17, of whom four were owner-occupiers. The farm sizes varied considerably, but the owner-occupied farms were of substantial acreage. The amount of arable had increased to 40 percent of the total acreage. There were 38 full-time male farm workers and 12 women, 16 male casual workers and six female. 1966 shows a return to conditions closer to those of 1903 than the rest of the century, with the number of farmers increased to 33 (but note that the National Farm Survey did not include smallholdings of 3 or less acres but the parish summaries did), of which 23 were under 15 acres. Arable accounted for 38 percent of the land, but sheep had returned in numbers, and poultry had increased to 5,768. The male full-time farm labour force had not changed since 1943 but the female full-time labour had been halved and there were only three male casual workers remaining.

Questions that can be asked about the parish summaries include the percentage of arable to grass, and the number of head of livestock per acre. The parish summaries allow for the exact detail on the amount of agricultural labour in an area. These are an excellent source for showing change over time.

Other information on farming can be found in MAF 7, which is the annual livestock survey arranged by county. This gives information on the breeds of livestock, the numbers of heifers in milk, and can be used in conjunction with breed books. Further details on land ownership can be found in MAF 9, which contains deeds and enfranchisements of land and manorial transfers. The entries describe the land and woods, but only from a manorial perspective. Information on where manorial material can be found is in the National Register of Archives Manorial Index. Economic details on farming activity are in MAF 15, the register of market prices.

The type of farming activity helps to determine how the landscape appears to the eye.

The Countryside Commission described the landscape as a 'visual impression created by structural elements in the countryside', and emphasised that the landscape was not an abstract art form.

The Commission drew up some useful guidelines by which to assess the landscape. Sensibly it pointed out that different people have different perceptions about the landscape. The example given to illustrate this is a hedge, which is seen by the farmer as a stock-proof barrier or a hindrance to machinery, to the naturalist as a haven for wild life, to the aesthetic observer as an object of texture and colour, and to the archaeologist and local historian as a dateable artefact that tells us about life in the past.[3] The local historian knows that although grubbing out hedges is injurious to wildlife and appals the conservationist, in many places the late twentieth-century landscape more closely resembles the landscape of the Middle Ages than that of the eighteenth and nineteenth centuries. It must be pointed out that the removal of hedgerows is not a new phenomenon. In 1918 an article appeared in the *Journal of the Ministry of Agriculture* on this subject. The local historian could use the removal of hedgerows as a case study to illustrate tensions in the countryside. Further information on the subject will be found in the town and country planning department of the county council records, but the local historian will also need information on land ownership to see whether the increase in hedgerow removal is related to the increase after 1918 of owner-occupation. Prior to this, many landlords who retained shooting rights over their tenant's land wished to keep hedgerows and copses as cover for game birds, and this too caused problems of access to the countryside. Examples of farming landscapes appear in **colour plates 18-19**.

The most up-to-date statistics on land ownership can be found in the agricultural census of 1988, which shows that the highest percentage of owner-occupation of farms was in Devon, Cumbria and North Yorkshire, but the largest-acreage farms were found in Norfolk and Northumberland. A study of parishes within these areas compared with others from outside would make a useful contribution to our understanding of the landscape.

Another phenomenon that the local historian can explore is the demise of the small farmer and the rise and fall of county council smallholdings. County councils started to acquire land for small tenancies during the second decade of the century. Details of these acquisitions will be found in the minutes and papers of county council smallholding and allotment committees.

By the latter half of the twentieth century, land use in the countryside was changing with the encroachment of towns and cities, the building of estates for commuters, the development of new towns for city overspill populations, and as a last ditch attempt to preserve the countryside, the designation of 'green belt' areas where building was not permitted. Increased mobility and the use of the countryside as a leisure area by city dwellers has led to considerable tensions over access. The 1949 Access to the Countryside Act made it compulsory for local authorities to keep maps and descriptions of footpaths in their area, and to give the public access to these records. The 1968 Countryside Act defined three classes of public rights of way:

1. Byways open to all forms of traffic.
2. Bridleways which horses are allowed to use.
3. Footpaths which only pedestrians can use.

The second and third categories have now been invaded by the mountain bike and scramble cycle, which has added to the tensions in the countryside. Most county councils have a special section in the county planning office that deals with footpaths and their maintenance. Parish councils are also responsible for overseeing the maintenance of footpaths in their parish and information will be found in parish council records, either as a separate class of record or in the minutes, which may also contain parish maps. It is possible to close the footpath entirely under the 1947 Town and Country Planning Act. The owner must announce this in advance, and this often leads to an inquiry, details of which can be found in the records of the crown court.

Footpaths and access to the countryside are also the concerns of voluntary bodies that have a history dating back to the mid-nineteenth century. County and parish footpath preservation societies have deposited items such as minutes, accounts, programmes of activities and correspondence in their county record offices. The records of government bodies such as the National Parks Commission can be found in the PRO COU 1, whilst the information on the regional commissions which have the day-to-day management of the parks can be found locally.

Another open space eagerly sought out by those in pursuit of leisure are commons. Originally the common provided resources for the community in the form of grazing and fuel rights, but most of these rights have been commuted to freedom of access and recreation. Since 1965 commons and village greens have been registered. The register of commons was compiled, and is kept by, the county council and should be available through the county record office. As the expectations of those living in and using the countryside have changed in the twentieth century so has the demographic structure of the village. Some villages in desirable areas are often deserted in the week or winter as the cottages are purchased as second homes. Other villages close to large towns or a commuter network have become dormitories with the more picturesque properties inhabited by newcomers. In one way this change has helped to keep the village alive, but it has also led to local changes. Often the original inhabitants are unable to afford the higher property prices determined by the higher salaries of the newcomers, with the result that they are pushed to the periphery into council housing, or forced to move away. The local historian can examine this problem through reference to the electoral register, noting where those bearing surnames found in the village for several generations can be found today. Oral history, especially reminiscences from the older generation will reveal where their family originally lived in the village.

A less emotional and more statistical approach to this aspect of rural life is to use the socio-economic groupings given in the 10 percent sample of the summary census returns and to relate these to other sources such as passenger traffic surveys. It is also possible to relate names in the electoral register back through the century in a longitudinal study, with additional information taken from school log books and parish magazines. A study for Lincolnshire by B.A. Holderness showed a 70 percent turnover of farming families within

80 *Rural craftsmen, the thatcher. Still from* Letter from East Anglia, *1952. (East Anglian Film Archive)*

three generations, but a stabilisation of farm occupation in the early 1960s.[4]

At the end of the twentieth century few agricultural labourers are found on farms. Their story can be traced through the records of the National Union of Agricultural Workers whose local branch records can be found in the county record office, as can the local branch records of the National Farmers Union.

Other changes in village life during the twentieth century include the disappearance of village craftsmen as seen in figure **80**, as their skills are no longer needed. They can be traced through a sequence of trade directories which may reveal that rather than disappearing, many adapted to change, thus the blacksmith's shop became the first garage, or the two operated side by side. One of the most important village resources is the local post office. Details of village post offices, the sub-post masters and mistresses, the areas covered and other information can be found in the Post Office Archives (**81**).

Once important in village life, the parish church is now much more secular, and where rivalry once existed between church and chapel, life in the village is more ecumenical. Many parishes are now part of a group ministry, details of which can be found in Diocesan Yearbooks, which may also give some indication on the size of the congregation.

In the small market towns craftsmen have disappeared in the late twentieth century, and each high street has a depressing uniformity with either shops boarded up or chain stores. Most shopping is done in the largest big town or out-of-town shopping centre, which can only be reached by car.

81 *Post woman, c.1915. (The Post Office)*

Does the twentieth century end with the same divisions between rich and poor as it began? Is the class element still found in local society and can it be defined by differences of cultural and material wealth and expectations? In studying the twentieth century perhaps the local historian can show that knowledge gained from the past can be used to plan for the future.

References

Chapter 1

1. BPP, Census of England and Wales, 1901, General Report, Cmnd., 2174,HMSO, 1904; BPP, Census of England and Wales, 1911 Administration Areas, Cmnd., 6258, HMSO, 1912; BPP Census of England and Wales, 1921, Preliminary Report, Cmnd., 1923; BPP, Census of England and Wales 1931, General Report, HMSO, 1950; General Register Office, Census 1951 England and Wales, HMSO, 1958; General Register Office, Census 1961 Great Britain, HMSO, 1968; Office of Population, Censuses and Surveys, Census 1971, England and Wales, HMSO, 1973; OPCS, Census 1981, Reports and County Reports Government Statistical Service, 1983; OPCS, 1991 Census, Government Statistical Service, 1993. (Note how the publishing body and the titles change over time)
2. Information on the orphanhood of children is found on Tables 24 and 24a, pp. 72-3 of the census county volumes.
3. BPP, Census of England and Wales, County of Cambridge, HMSO, 1903, p.v.
4. BPP, Census of England and Wales, 1911, Administrative Areas, p. 29.
5. CRO R55/11/7.
6. BRO X470/4.
7. CRO G/l/Xvb.
8. Mass Observation Archive, File Report 2485, The State of Matrimony, 1947.

Chapter 2

1. CRO, Cambridgeshire County Council, Minutes of the Public Health Committee, 1940–49; Cambridge Borough Archives, Minutes of the Public Health Committee, 1910–36; Minutes of the Maternity and child Welfare Sub-Committee, 1937.
2. CRO, Cambridge Borough Archives, Minutes of the Public Health Committee, September, 1938.
3. CRO, Cambridge Borough Archives, Health Visitors Report, 1906–13.
4. CRO, Cambridge Borough Archives, School Dental Service, Reports 1910–20; School Medical Inspector, Reports, 1910–20.
5. PRO, MH 66/1 and MH 66/283, p. 46.
6. Public Records Act 1958, Access to Hospital Records Circular, 2/Gen/33/33, pp. 1-2.
7. BRO, LF 58/2-3.
8. BRO HO: B/A 22.
9. Figures taken from R. Pinker, *English Hospital Statistics, 1861–1937*, 1966, p. 121.
10. BRO, BW M 2 .
11. BRO, NCR 1.
12. BRO, NM1.
13. BRO X 413/1-2.; Z 585/1-16;WMV 11/1-6; CRO, H. Landers, pharmacists, Records, 1880–1962.
14. British Red Cross Society, Voluntary Aid Department, Chippenham Division, List of Property, 1914.

Chapter 3

1. BPP, Census of England and Wales, Administrative Areas, Cmnd. 2174, 1911, p. xii.
2. *ibid.* Vol. 1. p. 169.
3 Figures of Tables 6 and 7 are taken from the appropriate county volumes of the Summary Census Returns of England and Wales, 1911.
4. *ibid.* County volume for Cambridgeshire.
5. Figures for Tables 6 and 7 taken from the county volumes of the Summary Census Returns England and Wales, 1961.
6. Figures for tables 12-15 taken from National Dwelling and Housing Survey, HMSO, 1978.
7. Ministry of Health, Annual Reports, HMSO, 1945–66.
8. Ibid.
9. PRO, HLG 49/260.
10. BRO UDA 6/1.
11. BRO, RDB WH 5/1(3)
12. SRO 1910 Nutfield Parish, Duties on Land Value Tax, 1910.
13. CRO, 470/075.

Chapter 4

1. CRO, R60/8/21.22.
2. CRO, Cambridgeshire County Council, Education Committee, Libraries Sub-committee, Minutes.
3. CRO Cambridge Borough Archives, Books Sub-committee, Minutes.

Chapter 5

1. C. Emsley, *The English Police*, 1991, e.g. p. 30.
2. *ibid.,* p. 88.
3. Home Office, Report of the Police Committee on Local Conditions of Service 1947, pp.3, 5, 11, 13.
4. BRO MICF 79 Bedfordshire County Constabulary, (Leighton Buzzard and Woburn division) Record of Crime Book, 1878–1934.
5. BRO, MICF 79, Bedfordshire County Constabulary, (Sandy Division), General Report Book, 1924–45.
6. BRO, MICF 79, Bedfordshire County Constabulary, (Dunstable), Register of Charges, 1887–1909.
7. BRO MICF 79 Bedfordshire County Constabulary, Record of Service Book, 1927–40.
8. BRO, BOR 9598. 150.
9. BRO, MCF 79, Bedford Borough Police, Register of grocers and Refreshment House Licences,1890–1946.
10. BRO, QER 20.
11. BPP, Criminal Registrar, Annual Report, 1903, p. 68.

Chapter 6

1. Figures taken from the Liquor Licensing Board for England and Wales, Annual Licensing Statistics, 1901, 1903, 1939, 1949, 1959, 1969.
2. CRO GK 176–177, 188.
3. East Anglian Film Archive, *Newsletter*, 'Aims of the Archive', 1996.
4. BRO, X 463/3.
5. CRO, P79/28/62.
6. CRO, P37/24/1.
7. CRO, P117/24/1.
8. CRO, R 54/30/2
9. BRO, X213.
10. CRO, 331/21.

Chapter 7

1. A. Smith, *The Wealth of Nations* 1776, 1986 ed. p. 251.
2. H.R. De Salis, *Canals and Navigable Rivers*, known as *Bradshaw's Canals and Navigable Rivers*, 1904, facsimile reprint, 1969.
3. British Transport Commission, Canals and Inland Waterways, Report of a Survey, HMSO, 1955, p. 39.
4. British Waterways Board, Recreational Use of Boats, Canals, Rivers and Reservoirs, Annual Count, 1967–71, HMS, 1971.
5. The Labour Party, The National Planning of Transport, 1939.
6. British Railways Board, Re-shaping British Railways, HMSO, 1963, pp.2, 4.
7. The Universal Directory of Railway Officials, p.11.
8. CUL Vickers PLC, 577, 1104, 1146.
9. Kelly's Directory for Suffolk, 1925, p. 469.
10. BRO, BOR 4/Ct/1/h, 4a, 10.
11. BRO, TL 32/34; TLX 4/3; TLO 11, Hi/Ts 1/4; TE 1 /3/1/; TE 1 3/4.
12. BRO, BOR/l/CT/7/1.

Chapter 8

1. M.E. Bulkley, Bibliographic Survey of Contemporary Sources for the Economic and Social History of the War, 1922; H. Hall, *British Archives and the Sources for the History of the World War*, 1925.
2. Hall, *op.cit.* pp. 397-8.
3. J. Winter, *The Great War and the British People,* CUP, 1985, p. 81.
4. CRO, Cambridge Borough Archives, Miscellaneous Bundle 213.
5. CRO, 331/21.
6. CRO, P150/24/1-2.
7. CRO 424/01.
8. CRO, Cambridgeshire Agricultural Executive Committee, Minutes, 1916-19.
9. CRO P150/3/13.
10. PRO INF 1/292.
11. J. Dow & M. Brown, *Evacuation to Westmoreland from Home and Abroad 1939-45*, 1946 p. 12; S. Isaacs ed. *The Cambridge Survey of Evacuation*, 1941; Cambridge Borough Council, War Emergency Committee, Evacuation Sub-committee, Minutes, 1939–45; Air Raid Precaution Committee, Minutes, 1938–45; BRO BOR L/Ca/1/7.
12. The Conditions of Service in the Home Guard, HMSO, 1942, p. 90.
13. CRO R 54/25/3.

Chapter 9

1. G. Bourne, *Change in the Village*, 1912; J. Connell, *The End of Tradition*, 1978.
2. The Countryside Commission, Non Agricultural Landscapes, 1974.
3. *op. cit.,* pp. 1-2.
4. B.A. Holderness 'Agriculture' in D. Mills ed. *Twentieth Century Lincolnshire*, 1989, pp. 53, 57.

Select bibliography

Unpublished Primary Sources

Bedfordshire County Record Office

BOR L/CT/1/1a-19a Luton Borough, Town Clerk, Luton Corporation Bus Service Accounts, Staffing, Routes.

BOR L/CT/7/1 Luton Borough, Town Clerk, Luton Municipal Airport, Income and Accounts, 1959–64.

BOR L/CT/7/7 Luton Borough Council, Report of the Committee on Tramways, 1908.

BRO 9598.150 Register of Fully Licensed Houses, 1900–1936.

Hi/Ts/1/4 Bedford Borough Council, Highway Sub-committee, Traffic Survey of Bromham Bridge, 1901.

HO: B/A22 Annual Report of Bedford County Hospital, 1947.

HO: BW M 2 Biggleswade Joint Hospital Board, Committee Minutes, 1922–1946.

LF 58/2-3 Records of Fairfield Hospital.

MICF 79 Bedford Borough Police, Beat Book.

MICF 79 Bedford Borough Police, Conduct Book, 1865–1930.

MICF 79 Bedford Borough Police, Register of Grocers and Refreshment House Licences, 1890–1946.

MICF 79 Bedfordshire County Constabulary, General Report Book, Sandy, 1914–1945.

MICF 79 Bedfordshire County Constabulary, Register of Charges, Dunstable 1887–1909.

MICF 79 Bedfordshire County Constabulary, Record of Crime Book, Leighton Buzzard and Woburn Division, 1878–1934.

MICF 79 Bedfordshire County Constabulary, Record of Service Book, 1927–1946.

NM1 Bedford Association of Midwives, Records, 1912–1947.

NCR1 Cardington Nursing Association, Records, 1900–1947.

QER 20 Bedfordshire Constabulary, Register of Chimney Sweeps, 1900–21.

RBD WH 5/1 (3) Biggleswade RDC, Overcrowding Survey, 1935.

R.O X463/3 Bedford Rugby Club, Records.

TE1 3/1 and 4 Bedfordshire County Council, Traffic Surveys of Watling Street, 1930, 1937.

TL 11 Licence Survey of Sharnbrook.

TLA 51 Licence Applications.

TLA 83-85 Vehicle Registration Cards.

TL1 32/34 Register of Licenses Issued.

UDA 6/1 Ampthill Urban District Council, Housing Committee Minutes, 1921–1948.

X 21/3 Oakley Hunt, Records.

X 413/1-24 Messrs. Taylor, Brawn and Flood, Chemists of Bedford, Records 1900–1937.
X 470/4 Records of T.H. Pacey, Undertakers Bedford, 1920–1939
X 843/51 Records of T.E. Neville, Undertakers of Luton.

Cambridgeshire County Record Office

Cambridge Borough Archives

Cam Conservators Papers Clayhithe Toll Book, 1904–1920.
Register of Boats, 1925–1934.
Cambridge Borough Court, Petty Sessions, Record Books.
Cambridge Borough Sessions, clerk of the peace, Letter Books, 1942.
Calendar of Prisoners, 1948–1963.
Chief Constable of the Borough of Cambridge, Annual Reports ,1933–1961.
Education Committee, Library Sub-committee, Minutes.
Fire Brigade and General Papers, 1900–1921.
Health Visitors Reports.
Housing and Town Planning Committee, Minutes, 1923–1949.
Miscellaneous Bundle 213.
Police Committee, Minutes, 1913–1914.
Public Health Committee, General Minutes.
Public Health Committee, Maternity and Child Welfare Committee, Minutes 1947–1954.
Public Works and Town Planning Committee, Minutes, 1928–1943.
Quarter Sessions Records, 1910–1941.
Register of Unfit Houses.
Sanitary Inspectors Journal, 1946–1961.
School Dental Service, Reports.
Slum Clearance File, 1937–1945.
Town Planning Committee, Minutes, 1913–1923.
War Emergency Committee, Minutes, 1938–1945.
Watch Committee Minutes, 1900–1921.

Cambridgeshire County Council

Education Committee, Library Sub-committee, minutes, 1981–1985.
Public Health and Housing Committee, minutes 1923–1948.
Theatres Committee, minutes, 1913–1933.
War Agricultural Executive Committee, minutes, 1918

Ely and Witchford Petty Sessions Division, Licensing Book under the 1909 Cinematographic Licensing Act.

331/21-28, Linton Parish Magazine, 1904–1920.
337/0.95 Gamlingay Land Tax Assessment, 1947–1949.
424/01 Swaffham Prior, Parish Diary 1914–18.
470/075 1910 Finance Act Valuation Book, Gamlingay.
GK 176/16, 177/5, 10, 13, 188/13, Hudsons Brewery Records.

G/L/XVb3 Linton, Board of Guardians, Return of All Births Registered, 1913–19, 1925–1941.
G/L/XVr 2-3 Linton, Vaccination Officers, Report Book 1907–1930.
Rate Book, 1910, 1934.
P 37/24/1 Caxton Cricket Club records, 1907–1911.
P 74/24/1 Melbourne Church Tennis Club, minute book , 1930–1952.
P 79/28/64 Grantchester Cricket Club Committee, minutes, lists of registered players, 1956–1960.
P 79/26/62 Grantchester Football Club, account book and fixtures, 1952–1956, 1983.
P 117/A-2 Disciplinary hearing on Madingley Rangers, 1975.
P 117/24/1 Melbourne Tennis Club record, 1930–1952.
P 150/24/1,2 Swaffham Prior, minutes of the proceedings of the Belgium Hospitality Committee, 1914–1915.
P 150/24/2-3 Report of the War Refugees Committee, 1917.
R 54/25/3 Girton Parish Invasion Committee, reports and minutes, 1942–44.
R 54/30/2 Linton Parish Council, minute book, 1900-1928.
R 55/11/7 Gamlingay, Burial Board, account book.
R 60/8/21.22 Harston School log book 1903-1959.

Cambridge University Library
Vickers PLC 577 Apprentice book, Barrow Yard, 1905-1948.
1104 Register of ships built in the Barrow Yard.
1146 Quotation book, Barrow Yard.

Mass Observation Archive
Diarist 5284
Diarist 5286
FR 2495 The State of Matrimony, 1947.
FR 3016, Outline Report on Drinking Habits, 1948.
TC Box 3/D Housing Satisfaction, Ipswich, 1941.

PRO
AN 25 Excursion Bill, A 63.
ED 2 Parish Files
ED 2/248 Parish File, Nutfield.
ED 7 Preliminary Statements.
ED 7/58 Preliminary Statement, Middleton, Lancs. 1910.
ED 18 Attendance Files.
ED 18/400 Attendance File, Bath 1929-32.
ED 18/641 Attendance File, Bath, 1936.
ED 60 Staffing Files.
ED 60/5/193B(i) Staffing File, Jarrow, 1927-36.
ED 73/3 University of Cambridge, Board of Extra-Mural Studies, File, 1911-1935.
ED 196 Inspectors Reports.

ED 196/5 Inspectors Report on Linton Village College, 1947.
HLG 4 Planing Schemes, 1905-51.
HLG 14 Sanctions for local authority housing loans.
INF 1 2929 Committee on Evacuation, Reports.
IR 58 Field Books.
IR 58/69667 Field Book, Nutfield, 1910.
IR 58/16547 Field Book, Gamlingay, 1910.
MAF 7 Livestock Survey.
MAF 7/10 Livestock Survey, Cambridgeshire, 1913.
MAF 7/17 Livestock Survey, Durham, 1913.
MAF 32 National Farm Survey.
MAF 32/811/82 National Farm Survey, Gamlingay.
MAF 32/1050/128 National Farm Survey, Nutfield.
MAF 68 Parish Summaries.
MAF 68/1999 Parish Summary, Gamlingay, 1903.
MAF 68/2028 Parish Summary, Nutfield, 1903.
MAF 68/3153 Parish Summary, Nutfield, 1923.
MAF 68/4065 Parish Summary, Nutfield, 1943
MAF 68/4825 Parish Summary, Nutfield, 1963.
MAF 73/40 no 35 National Farm Survey, Map of Nutfield.
MH 66/1 County Report on Bedfordshire, 1937.
MH 66/823 Report on the Municipal Borough of Poole, 1937.
MH 67 Joint Hospital Board Reports.
MT 121/7 File M6 Preston By-pass Section.

Surrey County Record Office

CC 99/17/2 Surrey County Council, Smallholdings and Allotments Committee, Minutes 1912-1936.
2333/7/7/2 Kings Mill Estate, Nutfield, Notice to A. Howick of resumption of the possession of land, 1911.
2333/7/7/5 Kings Mill Estate, Nutfield, Sale Particulars. Letter from County Land Agent, 2 November 1911.
2415/1/25 Finance Act 1910 Valuation Book, Nutfield.
2833 Deeds of Kings Mill, Nutfield, 1907-1911.

Published Primary Sources

Anglia Railways Annual Report, 1995.
Board of Trade, Handbook on Canals, 1918.
H. Bosanquet, *Social Conditions in Provincial Towns*, 1912.
G. Bourne, *Change in the Village*, 1912.
British Parliamentary Papers, Census of England and Wales 1901.
General report and county volumes, 1904.
Census of England and Wales, 1911.
Administrative areas and county volumes, 1912.

Census of England and Wales, 1921.
Preliminary report and county volumes, 1923.
Census of England and Wales, 1931.
General report and county volumes, 1950.
Criminal Registrar's report, 1903.
British Railways, Eastern Region, staff directives, 1977.
British Tourist Authority survey of regional tourism, 1982.
British Transport Commission, canals and inland waterways, report of the Board of Survey, 1955.
British Waterways Board, Recreational Use of Boats, Canals, Rivers and Reservoirs, Annual Count 1967–71, 1971.
M.E. Bulkley, Bibliographical Survey of Contemporary Sources for the Economic and Social History of the War, 1922.
Cambridge and District Colts League, Regulations, 1977.
Cambridge Borough Police, Instructions to Special Constables, 1915.
Cambridge Evening News.
Cambridgeshire County Council, An Historical Account of Air Raid Precautions 1935-45, 1946.
Cambridgeshire County Council, Research and Information Unit, Population Estimates 1971-84, 1985.
H. De Salis, *Canals and Navigable Rivers*, 1904, facsimile reprint,1969.
J. Dow & M. Brown, *Evacuation to Westmoreland from Home and Abroad*,1946.
East Anglian Regional Health Authority, Minutes, 1994.
General Register Office, Census 1951 England and Wales,
County Volumes, 1958.
Census 1961 Great Britain, General Report, 1968.
Government Statistical Census, 1991, 1993.
H. Hall, *British Archives and the Sources for the History of the War*, 1925.
Home Office, Report of the Police Council — Local Conditions of Service for Police, 1947.
S. Isaacs, ed. The Cambridge Evacuation Survey, 1941.
Kelly's Directory, Suffolk, 1925.
Labour Party, The National Planning of Transport, 1939.
Liquor Licensing Board Annual Licensing Statistics.
Ministry of Agriculture, A Century of Agricultural Statistics 1888–1988, 1967.
Office of Population, Censuses and Survey Census 1971, England and Wales, 1973.
Census 1981, Reports and County Volumes, 1983.
Household Survey, 1977.
National Dwelling and Housing Survey, 1978.
R. Padley & M. Cole, eds. Evacuation Survey, 1940.
Public Records Act, 1958.
Access to Hospital Records Circular 2/Gen/33/33.
Red Cross, Chippenham Division, Cambridgeshire, List of Property, 1914.
Red Cross, VAD Auxiliary Hospitals, 1915.

Universal Directory of Railway Officials, 1925.
War Office, Conditions of Service in the Home Guard, 1942.
Regulations of the Home Guard, 1942.
Williams Cambridge and District Rail Guide, 1919–47.

Published Sources — Books

J. Benson, *Prime Time – A History of the Middle Aged in Twentieth-Century Britain*, 1997.
J. Connell, *The End of Tradition,* 1978.
Countryside Commission, *Non-Agricultural Landscapes*, 1974.
C. Emsley, *The English Police,* 1991.
J. R. Gillis, *A World of Their Own Making*, 1997.
H. Howgrave, *The Metropolitan Police at War,* 1947.
A. Land, R. Lowe & N. Whiteside, *The development of the Welfare State. A guide to documents in the PRO,* Public Record Office Handbook, No. 25, 1992.
S. Mackenzie, *The Home Guard,* 1995.
H. Meller, *Town plans and society in Modern Britain*, 1997.
D. Mills, ed. *Twentieth Century Lincolnshire,* History of Lincs. Committee, 1989.
A. Morton, *Education and the State from 1833.* PRO Readers' Guide No. 18, 1997.
D. Phillips & A. Williams, *Rural Britain. A Social Geography*, 1984.
R. Pinker, *English Hospital Statistics 1861–1938,* 1966.
E. Roberts, *Women and Families, An Oral History 1940-70*, 1995.
B. Short, *Land and Society in Edwardian Britain*, 1997.
J. Steadman, *Portsmouth Reborn, Destruction and Reconstruction 1939–74*, Portsmouth City Museum, 1995.
E. Wilkinson, *The Town that was Murdered, The Life Story of Jarrow*. 1939.
J. Winter, *The Great War and the British People,* 1986.

Published Sources — Articles

B.A. Holderness, 'Agriculture' in D. Mills ed., *Twentieth Century Lincolnshire* History of Lincs. Committee, 1989, pp. 37-70.
N. Moorson, 'Planning for the Post-War Redevelopment of Middlesborough', *Local History Magazine,* No. 50, July-August, 1995, pp. 7-15.
B.N.A. Wale, 'The Removal of Hedgerows', *Journal of the Ministry of Agriculture,* 1918, pp. 1411–24.

Useful addresses

Often the local historian will need to search for information in archives other than the county record office, local studies library, or Public Record Office. These records can be located in:

J. Foster and J. Shepherd, *British Archives: A guide to the Archive Resources of UK*, 3rd ed. 1995.

This publication, which should be available in any large reference library, gives the addresses, telephone numbers, opening hours, and access details of archives. It describes the historical background to the archives, its acquisitions policy, its major holdings, facilities and publications.

The collections at the addresses below contain records of interest to local historians:

Brewers & Licensed Retailers Association
42 Portman Square
London W1H 0BB

British and Foreign School Society Archive Centre
West London Institute of Higher Ed.
Lancaster House
Borough Road
Isleworth TW7 5DU

Byways and Bridleways Trust
The Granary
Charlcutt
Calne, Wilts SN11 9HZ

Charity Commission
St Alban's House
57/60 Haymarket
London SW1Y 4QX

Commons Commission
Golden Cross House
Duncannon Street
London WC2

Commons, Open Space & Footpath Preservation Society
25a Bell Street
Henley-on-Thames
Oxfordshire

Council for the Preservation of Rural England
4 Hobart Place
London SW1 0HT

Family Records Centre
1 Myddelton Street
London EC1

Football Association
16 Lancaster Gate
London W2 3LW

Girls Public Day School Trust
26 Queen Anne's Gate
London SW1H 9AN

Institute of Brewing
33 Clarges Street
London W1Y 8EE

Labour History Archive
National Museum
103 Princess Street
Manchester M1 6DD

National Maritime Museum
Romney Road
Greenwich
SE10 9NF

National Railway Museum
Leeman Road
York YO2 4XJ

Police History Society
18 Cornec Close
Leigh-on-Sea
Essex SS9 5EN

Public Record Office
Ruskin Avenue
Kew

Registrar General of Shipping and Seamen
Anchor House
Cheviot Close
Parc Ty Glas
Llanishen
Cardiff CF4 5JA

The BP Archive
The Library
University of Warwick
Coventry CV4 7AL

The archives are open to serious researchers by prior appointment with the Senior Archivist.

Oil and petroleum company records are a class of records peculiar to the twentieth century. The BP Archive is a good example of the type of material to be found in such archives.

BP was the result of an initiative by William Knox D'Arcy who in 1901 was granted a 60-year concession by the Shah of Persia for the exploration of oil in his country. In 1908 oil was discovered in quantity and the Anglo-Persian Oil Company was founded in 1909. This became the Iranian Oil Company in 1935, and the British Petroleum Company in 1954.

Although much of the company archive refers to business overseas and to the running of the company, there is material in it which is of interest to local historians as not only did the oil industry create a new series of records but also new employment opportunities. The archive includes information on staff and activities in BP works in the UK, and material on the distribution of petroleum. An understanding of the mechanics of the latter is essential for a local historian working on the local economics of transport in the twentieth century. House journals contain valuable social information, and posters and photographs illustrate the development of the petroleum industry and the people who worked in it.

Film Archives

When the twentieth century began, the use of film was still in its infancy, but its potential as a record of national and local events was realised, and professional and amateur cameramen were present at these events. A collection of films of the First World War was placed in an archive in 1919 and is now part of the Imperial War Museum Film and Video Archive. The second film archive was the National Film Archive formed in 1935 — now the National Film and TV Archive.

Thanks to the efforts of regional film archives these unique records of life in the twentieth century have been preserved and made accessible. The first film archive to be formed was the East Anglian Film Archive founded in 1976. It aims to 'search and preserve moving pictures, either on film or videotape, which show life and work', most importantly where copyright allows accessibility. The archive covers the counties of Bedfordshire, Cambridgeshire, Essex, Hertfordshire, Norfolk, and Suffolk and is housed in the University of East Anglia. In 1996 the archive contained 20,000 cans of film covering every aspect of life in East Anglia and ranging in date from 1896 to the 1990s. Fig **96** is a still from the archive.

The second film archive to be formed was the North West Film Archive founded in 1977. This too contains a wide range of material dating from 1896 to the present day. Much of this material covers the urban and industrial society of the northwest, and thus makes an interesting contrast with the more rural society of East Anglia.

A further film archive covering Britain at war can be found in the Imperial War Museum.

East Anglian Film Archive
University of East Anglia
Norwich NR4 7TJ

North West Film Archive
Manchester Metropolitan Museum
Minshull House
47-49 Chorlton St
Manchester M1 3EU

Modern Records Centre
The Library
University of Warwick
Coventry
CV4 7AL

Tel. 01203 514219
Fax 01203 524211
(Advanced booking advised)
Open to all serious researchers, access on a few days' notice (**colour plate 20**).

The Modern Records Centre was formed in 1973 in order to collect records covering industrial relations and politics. The archive also holds social and economic records of interest to the local historian. These include records of trade unions and firms from the West Midlands and elsewhere. For example, Fakenham Enterprises (Mss 30), Macclesfield Silk and Textiles Ltd (Mss 162), Bristol Unity Players (Mss 212) and the records of the East Midlands region of the Labour Party. There are also local branch records of unions such as the Transport Salaried Staff Association for Wisbech from 1908–1956 (Mss 55).

The records of the national, political, and industrial concerns such as the Amalgamated Engineers Union, Trades Union Congress or the Confederation of British Industry held in the archive, will enable the local historian to place local studies within a national context, and look at local reactions to decisions taken at a national level.

The Mass Observation Archive

The Library
University of Sussex
Falmer
Brighton
BN1 9QL

Mass Observation was founded in 1937 with the aim of studying the everyday lives of ordinary people through the observations and interviews of paid researchers and a panel of volunteers who kept diaries and responded to monthly questionnaires. The whole archive is especially useful to local historians as it can be accessed by location as well as person and subject. There are also publications based on Mass Observation material which make an excellent starting point for research.

The earliest work of Mass Observation was the 'Worktown Study' of 1937–40, which was based on Bolton and Blackpool and was a blanket coverage of all aspects of life. The records of this study include over 1800 photographs.

The returns of the paid researchers can be found in the file reports, which are typewritten reports summarising their observations. These are particularly useful for observations of everyday life during the Second World War, and cover topics such as morale, wartime shopping, and wartime Christmases. The local historian working on a village will be interested in file reports 1995, 2487, which are a survey of three villages in Somerset taken during the war. Some of the material was published in 1947 as *An Exmoor Village,* by W.J. Turner. Further evidence can be found in the Topic Collections Town and District Surveys 1938-49. These reveal that the paid investigator was not always objective, and brought middle-class value judgements into a working-class environment. For example the Luccombe investigator added 'inevitable' to the inventory of pictures in a Luccombe cottage which included the Royal Family, the Monarch of the Glen and the Devon and Somerset Hunt, and described the furniture as 'poor quality'. (TC Town and District Surveys, 1938-49. Box 6 File, B pp. 2, 4-5).

As well as the Topic Collection and file reports, also available are 'day surveys', which asked volunteers to keep an accurate record of everything they did on the 12th of each month. Volunteers were also asked to answer questionnaires on important issues. These are 'directive replies' and cover subjects such as class and housing. A further 500 volunteers kept diaries covering the period 1939-63.

The whole adds up to a unique record of life in the mid-twentieth century. The example below is of especial interest to local and family historians working on naming practices for any period as it illustrates the processes that go into naming a child and attitudes towards names.

File Report 2392 is a report on attitudes to names and ancestry in 1946. 200 replies showed that 50 percent were named after a relative or friend, 11 percent after a well-known person,

21 percent chosen because the parents liked the name, and the rest did not know why they had their name. Most were called by their proper name rather than a nickname. The report reveals that some names suggest stereotypes. Thus Adrian, Brian, and Trevor were seen as being middle-class names; Michael, David, and Joan, white-collar names; Daisy, Annie, Ethel, Cecil, and Horace, working-class names. The most popular girls' names were Elizabeth, Margaret, and Mary. Sarah, Jane, and Susan were unpopular, as were all flower names. Percy, Cyril, and Bert were unpopular boys' names, but the inevitable John, which had been the most popular name for centuries was still popular, along with James and David.

Six percent of the respondents denied all knowledge of their ancestors, or displayed any interest. The rest were interested to know who their ancestors were, and where they came from. They are the family historians of today.

The Post Office Archives

Freeling House
Mount Pleasant Compound
London EC1A 1BB
(The search room is shown in **colour plate 21.)**

An understanding of the activities of the post office and postal service in town or village is essential for the local historian working on the social and economic dimension of an area. The Post Office Archives have a collection of records, which range from the beginning of the postal service up to the late twentieth century. POST 1-2 cover all levels of staff employed by the Post Office from appointments, salary, promotion, and sick leave, to pensions and death gratuities. From these, the local historian can trace the careers of staff, from the Postmaster General to the village sub-postmistress, and (of importance to the village historian), the rise and fall of the village post office.

One of the prime functions of the Post Office is the delivery of mail, which can be traced through a reconstruction of the post rounds. POST 17 deals with the circulation and sorting of post.

1.Primary Sorting sends outward items into large towns for dispatch to divisional sorting points.
2.The mail is sorted at divisional level.
3.It is taken by a postman or postwoman, either by foot, bicycle, or van.

POST 21 contains maps of postal areas, and POST 13, details of air post.

Other material covers packet boats, the travelling post office – including details of its rolling stock, postage rates, rules for operating a post office, plans of post offices and other buildings, and a file on the Great Train Robbery. Much social history is contained in house journals, which show the post office staff at work and play.

The archives are covered by the Public Records Acts of 1958 and 1967, so that some of the more recent records are closed, but the whole is an important resource for the local historian.

Index